Here are the most important commands, all in one place, so that once you've read the book and practiced using the commands, you'll have them at your fingertips.

File Management Commands

Command...	What it does...
ls	Lists your files
ls -a	Lists all your files
ls -l	Lists your files in a long format
rm	Removes a file
rm -r	Double-checks with you before removing a file
mkdir	Makes a directory
cd	Changes to a directory
cd ..	Moves up one directory
rmdir	Removes a directory
rmdir -i	Double-checks with you before removing a directory
mv	Moves a file into a directory, or renames a file
cp	Copies a file
rm	Removes (deletes) a file
pwd	Tells you where you are

Printing Commands

Command...	What it does...
lp	Prints a file to the default printer
lp -d	Prints a file to a specific printer
lpstat -d	Shows the name of the default printer
lpstat	Tells you where your file is in the print queue
lpr	Works like lp; might be available on your computer system
cancel	Cancels a printout if you change your mind

File Security Commands

Command...	What it does...
login	Prompts you for your login id
passwd	Lets you change your password
id	Tells you who you are
who	Tells you who else is logged in
w	Tells you who else is logged in and what they are doing
finger	Tells you more info about other logged-in users
exit	Logs you out
Ctrl-d	Logs you out
logout	Logs you out

File Ownership Commands

Command...	What it does...
chmod	Changes file permissions for certain classes of users
chown	Changes the owner of the file
chgrp	Changes the primary group affiliation of the file's owner

File Creation Commands

Command...	What it does...
vi	Uses the visual editor to create a file
cat	Uses the concatenate command to create a file
touch	Creates an empty file, or updates the date on an existing file

Totally Cool Commands

Command...	What it does...
grep	Searches through files looking for the character string that you specify
find	Searches through the file system looking for files or directories that you've lost
sort	Sorts the data in a file by the first character of each line
ps	Lists all of your processes on-screen, so you can see what you're doing
alias	Lets you change the names of commands to suit you
history	Lists the last 40 or so commands you've typed, so you can repeat commands if you want

Communication Commands

Command...	What it does...
mail	Lets you read your mail or send new messages
gopher	Lets you tunnel through the Internet
telnet	Lets you log in to other computers
ftp	Lets you transfer files between computers
rn	Lets you read news from around the corner or around the world

Information-Gathering Commands

Command...	What it does...
man	Brings up the man page (on-line manual) for a specified command
man -k	Brings up keyword information on a specified topic

I HATE
UNIX®

Karla Saari Kitalong

I Hate UNIX

Copyright © 1994 by Que® Corporation.

Library of Congress Catalog No.: 94-65141

ISBN: 1-56529-620-6

97 96 95 94   6 5 4 3 2 1

Interpretation of the printing code: the rightmost double-digit number is the year of the book's printing; the rightmost single-digit number, the number of the book's printing. For example, a printing code of 94-1 shows that the first printing of the book occurred in 1994.

Screens reproductions in this book were created by using Collage Compute from Inner Media, Inc., Hollis, NH.

I Hate UNIX is based on UNIX System V.

Publisher: David P. Ewing

Associate Publisher: Michael Miller

Managing Editor: Michael Cunningham

Marketing Manager: Ray Robinson

Dedication

To my mom. She doesn't understand the work I do, but without her encouragement, I wouldn't be doing it.

I HATE UNIX!

Credits

Publishing Director
Joseph B. Wikert

Publishing Manager
Brad R. Koch

Acquisitions Editor
Sarah Browning

Product Director
Robin Drake

Production Editor
Linda Seifert

Editors
Lori Cates
Susan M. Dunn
Susan Ross Moore

Technical Editor
Pete Holsberg

Book Designer
Amy Peppler-Adams

Cover Designer
Tim Amrhein

Cover Illustration
Jeff MacNelly

Production Team
Angela Bannan
Steph Davis
Meshell Dinn
Brook Farling
Beth Lewis
Linda Quigley
Caroline Roop
Nanci Sears Perry
Becky Tapley
Sue VandeWalle
Donna Winter
Michelle Worthington

Indexer
Rebecca Mayfield

Editorial Assistant
Michelle Williams

Composed in *Goudy* and *MCPdigital* by Que Corporation.

About the Author

Karla Saari Kitalong discovered computers long after she reached adulthood. After struggling for two years with a recalcitrant mainframe—and ultimately winning—Kitalong came to the conclusion that computers must be a joke. Since then, her attitude toward the cocky machines has vastly improved. Today, Karla can be found living in the far reaches of Upper Michigan, near the end of that long, narrow finger of land that juts out into Lake Superior. She works as a computer specialist at Michigan Technological University, and is pursuing a Ph.D. in Rhetoric and Technical Communication. She is married with two nearly grown children.

I HATE UNIX!

Acknowledgments

Somewhere in this book, I said that no one learns UNIX completely solo. The same is true for writing a book about UNIX. Without the support and help of a bunch of people, this book would be just a gleam in my eye.

At Que: I've never worked with a more professional, hard-working bunch of people. I'm sure they did more behind the scenes than I know about, but I'd like to mention a few things here. Sarah Browning kept me on my toes about deadlines. Brad Koch helped develop the original outline and always asked about the Upper Michigan weather when he called. Robin Drake, Linda Seifert, and the rest of the editorial staff, caught a myriad of linguistic and logical lapses, thereby saving this book from a career as a doorstop. Pete Holsberg, the technical editor, helped me remember what is humorous about UNIX and lent me the benefit of his years of experience.

On the Home Front: Tino has put up with a lot. For nearly a quarter-century, he's been married to someone who routinely takes on four times as many projects as she can possibly accomplish. If that's not bad enough, this overzealous person—who shall remain nameless—expects him to pick up the slack around the house, serve as her personal complaint department when things aren't going well, and hang out alone every night and weekend. The phrase "the wind beneath my wings" comes easily to mind.

We have two wonderful children. Ann, on the verge of starting her own life, is taking new responsibilities in stride and learning the valuable lesson that offers of help are not always criticisms. Jim, the teenager in the household, excels in school and in life and handles parental interrogation with aplomb. We've been lucky—and their stability makes my writing possible.

Thanks to my mother, Irma, and my late father, Carl, who taught me the value of hard work and good old-fashioned Finnish *sisu* (the ability to keep going in the face of seemingly insurmountable obstacles). Just so you know, I finally understand why you made me go to college when all I wanted was to be a bum after I graduated from high school. My parents have done well. Of the four children they raised, three—my sisters, Karen and Kris, and my brother, Kevin—turned out normal. I'm the only weird-o in the bunch. Three out of four isn't bad!

At Work: Once, during an important meeting with my boss, Cindy Selfe, and three or four colleagues, I listened, expressed opinions, and corrected *I Hate UNIX* pages all at the same time. This level of preoccupation was typical during the months that I spent writing this book. I work with a great bunch of people, all of whom have prodded this project along in one way or another. Thanks to everyone I see in my daily travels. You may not know it, but you're all in this book, somewhere!

Trademark Acknowledgments

All terms mentioned in this book that are known to be trademarks or service marks have been appropriately capitalized. Que cannot attest to the accuracy of this information. Use of a term in this book should not be regarded as affecting the validity of any trademark or service mark.

UNIX is a registered trademark of Univel.

Contents at a Glance

Table of Contents

12 Somewhere around a Dozen Useful Commands   161

IV Private and Public Information: Permissions   167

13 Mother May I? Permissions and How They Work   169

Introduction

"I've forgotten that command—again!!!"

"I know I saved that file, but now I can't find it!!"

"I *hate* UNIX!"

"#$?/%@!"

his book about UNIX is for people like you and me—we have to use UNIX, but it has all those stupid little commands with their nit-picky little options. All we want to do is get our work done as smoothly and painlessly as possible.

Before you get too far along in this book, you'll notice that it has an attitude: "Computers have one purpose in life—to make us look good. But computers invariably do just the opposite, unless we show them who's boss." This is the book you need to help you gain the upper hand over UNIX.

Many UNIX books are written for people who already know a lot about computers. They like to write programs, have the memory of an elephant, and have a lot of time to explore and practice with their computer. When I was writing this book, I tried to picture a computer user like myself. Here's what I'm like—does it sound like you?

✔ Because I'm pretty smart, I can tell when I'm being patronized, even by a computer book. I hate when inanimate objects patronize me.

✔ I don't have much spare time to devote to learning UNIX or any other computer system—but I have little choice. Computers are essential to my daily routine.

✔ I'm not a programmer, but some of my day-to-day work involves helping to run my department's computer system. Someone's got to do it! I have a colleague who's a programmer, so I don't have to figure out everything on my own. But I need UNIX, because I can't run for help every time I need to get something done.

I Hate UNIX! is the book I needed when I was learning UNIX. It includes high-powered commands that programmers use, but it explains how *you* can use them to get *your* work done. It sorts out your immediate needs from your long-term, enrichment needs. You'll learn enough UNIX to be productive, to avoid looking like a fool in front of your colleagues, and to know when you're ready to move on to more advanced concepts.

With the help of this book, you can learn UNIX commands to make your computer—that inert mass of plastic and silicon—perform for you. Soon, at your urging, your computer will be leaping taller buildings, breaking new Olympic records, and making you look good, while you sit back and collect the kudos.

Ready to get started? Wait a minute—skim the next section for some important information about how this book is laid out.

About This Book's Icons (What those little pictures really mean)

You're reading this book because you want a straightforward, non-technical UNIX learning experience. But you're not going to get off that easily. You're going to have to learn some technical buzzwords, off-beat computer functions, and big, bad no-no's. That's why you see a bunch of little pictures scattered throughout this book.

The icons identify some useful information that you can get along without, but might not want to.

Here are the pictures and what they mean:

TIP

This icon alerts you to shortcuts, tricks, and time-savers.

BUZZWORDS

This icon warns you that you're about to learn an impressive technobabble word.

"I HATE THIS!"

This icon brings you back to reality. Just when you think you're getting a handle on UNIX's quirks, you are reminded of the frustrating, annoying things it does.

CAUTION

This icon says: You're treading on dangerous turf here. Proceed carefully!

EXPERTS ONLY

This icon flags the really technical stuff. If there was a UNIX trivia game, reading these sections would help you excel.

PART I

UNIX and You: Getting Started

Includes:

CHAPTER 1

What To Do First

IN A NUTSHELL

- ▼ Introduction to UNIXland
- ▼ Understanding your computer
- ▼ Searching for your identity
- ▼ Logging in
- ▼ Exploring UNIXland
- ▼ Passwords
- ▼ Logging out

Welcome to UNIXland. You may have heard that it's an inhospitable place, with a complex, cryptic native language that no one, especially you, can learn. Well, that's only partly true.

UNIXland—Your First Stop on the Information Highway

First of all, UNIXland isn't a real place. It's just a computer operating system. But I find that when I'm learning about a new computer system, it helps to think about it as a new culture, with customs that may not make sense to me, but that are perfectly logical to the inhabitants. Think about the kinds of transitions that are required when you move to a new city, start a new job, or visit a foreign country. Similar transitions are required to learn to navigate the terrain and culture of UNIXland. You may have heard that UNIXland is full of complexity and crypticness. But don't worry. You don't have to emigrate to UNIXland; in fact, you only have to go there once in a while. A handful of commands gets you started, just like a handful of phrases gets you through most visits to other cultures. After a while, you begin to notice some patterns; after all, the creators of UNIXland were humans, like you and me.

Anyway, this book is your guide to UNIXland. Enough beating around the bush—let's get started.

What the heck is UNIX, anyway?

It was back in the summer of 1988 that I first started to work with UNIX. When I visited my sister, she asked me how work was going. I told her that we were getting some new computers, and that I was going to have to learn about UNIX. She responded, "You **would** be interested in eunuchs!" OK, I admit it, my sister thinks I'm weird. She was not at all surprised that I had a job learning about eunuchs. Since then, she, too, has gained some experience with UNIX-based computers, but she still thinks I'm odd.

Well, you now know that UNIX is not a neutered man who works in a harem. But I haven't told you what it is. Here goes. It's a computer operating system. In your previous run-ins with computers, you may have heard of DOS, an operating system that runs on most personal computers. UNIX is another operating system that runs on many different kinds of computers.

An operating system like UNIX is just a special type of computer program whose job it is to control how the computer works. Some of the tasks under the operating system's control include how other programs (like word processors) function, how printers and terminals behave, and how the computer interacts with you, the user.

Certain types of operating systems are particularly well suited to doing certain types of tasks; one of UNIX's strengths is that it makes it possible for several people to simultaneously use one central computer to do their work.

Understanding Your Computer
(It's not just a paperweight anymore)

UNIX works on many different kinds of computers. It is a mistake to say, "Turn on your computer," because, depending on the kind of computer you have, that might not be such a good idea. One way or another, though, you've got to get power to your computer.

CAUTION

Since UNIX-based computers are often part of a network, you could make a mess if you turn your computer on or off incorrectly. Read this chapter, or talk to your resident expert (if you have one) before touching the power switch.

Workstations

You should NEVER turn a workstation off. If it is off when you start, you need a specialist to tell you how to turn it on. This is called Progress.

How to find out if your computer is a workstation

✔ Does your computer appear to be turned off? Find the key on your keyboard that's labeled "Enter," "Return," or "Send" and press it once. If the screen lights up and a `login:` prompt appears, you're probably using a workstation.

✔ Even if the screen doesn't light up, you may have a workstation. Sometimes the *CPU* (the computer's brains, contained in the big box that may be part of your computer) and the *monitor* (the thing that looks like a TV) must be turned on separately. Don't touch the CPU power switch, but do check for a power switch on the front, side, or back of the monitor. Flip it and see what happens—just because there's no light in the window, doesn't mean that nobody's home.

✔ Is the word "Sun," "Sparc," or "Apollo" written on the front of your computer? These are common workstation brand names. If your computer has one of these common brand names, it might be a workstation. There are many other brands of workstations, so don't use brand name as your only clue.

✔ Did someone in charge of computers where you work (perhaps a person sporting a pocket protector or a propeller-head beanie) tell you that your machine is a workstation? These sort of people use technical terms very precisely, so it's usually safe to believe what they say, even if you don't understand it. If that person can help, you are in luck. He or she can explain how your computer communicates with UNIX and tell you what (and especially what NOT) to do.

If your computer is not a workstation, your job may become easier or harder, depending on what you have to do.

Pros and cons of workstations

✔ *Pro:* Workstations can help you avoid getting down and dirty with UNIX. A *graphical user interface* (GUI, often pronounced "gooey") running on a workstation can make your work go more smoothly. Chapter 5 tells you all about this.

✔ *Con:* If you have a GUI, you may miss out on knowing HOW and WHY things work as they do. You have to know *some* UNIX to be truly productive.

✔ *Pro:* If your company has several (3 to 3,000) workstations, someone in a position of power might have hired a professional UNIX lover to be responsible for the care and feeding of the computers. This person is your shield against the gory innards of UNIX.

continues

Pros and cons of workstations (continued)

✔ *Con:* You have to talk to that professional UNIX lover whenever you need something done to your computer. Professional UNIX lovers do not like talking to ordinary mortals. They are at their best when talking one-on-one with the computer, and may try to make you feel stupid so you leave them alone with their technology.

If you haven't figured out by this time if your computer is a workstation, ask someone. Since workstations shouldn't be turned on and off at random, you have to know if your computer is a workstation to continue.

PCs and Terminals

OK, so what if your computer isn't a workstation? Then it is either a PC, a dumb terminal, an intelligent terminal, or a PC acting like a dumb or intelligent terminal.

BUZZWORDS

DUMB TERMINAL, INTELLIGENT TERMINAL, and PC

A *dumb terminal* lets you communicate directly with a central computer running UNIX. A dumb terminal consists of a keyboard, a monitor, and some wires. It has no CPU or disks of its own; it uses the memory and processing power of the central computer to which it's connected.

An *intelligent terminal* (or PC acting like one) lets you transfer information to and from the central UNIX machine to local disks (disks attached directly to the terminal). Once the information has been transferred to the local disks, you can work with it as though it were local information, and store it back on the central computer when you have finished with it.

PC stands for *personal computer*. The most common types of PCs are IBM-compatibles and Macintoshes. A PC can run its own version of UNIX, or it can be connected as a dumb terminal to a central computer. In the latter case, the disks and memory attached to the PC are mostly ignored, and the PC relies on the memory and processing power of the central computer.

Dumb terminals can be turned on and off at will—look for a switch somewhere on the front, side, or back of the computer. Sometimes the CPU and the monitor must be turned on and off individually. PCs running UNIX in stand-alone mode (not connected to a network) may be turned on and off at will, but a special shut-down procedure may be required.

BUZZWORDS

CPU and MONITOR

The *CPU* (short for *Central Processing Unit*) is the thinking part of a computer. On a PC, the CPU is often contained in a rectangular box, along with disk drives, connectors, and other stuff.

The *monitor* is the part of your computer that looks like a TV. Some people call it the *display* or *screen*.

If you can't figure out how to turn on your computer, or if you're not sure whether you have a PC, a dumb terminal, or a workstation, ask around a little bit. Probably someone you work with can help you find out if you have to turn on your computer in a certain way. Instead of making you sound like a fool, this question makes others recognize that you know UNIX is fussy about these things.

Whew. When you finally have your computer turned on, some messages are likely to appear on-screen. These messages are different on different UNIX systems, but the last thing you see is this word

```
login:
```

That's called a prompt and its appearance is a good sign. It means UNIX is ready to recognize you and let you do your work.

If you don't see a login prompt, it probably means that you must type some commands to start UNIX on your computer, or to connect your PC or dumb terminal to a larger computer that runs UNIX. The specific commands you type vary depending on the hardware and software you are using; it would take the remaining pages in this book to list them all, if we even knew what all of them were. Rest assured that if the commands are this tough to figure out, there's got to be someone around who knows! Get chummy with that person right now, and save yourself a lot of headaches.

"I HATE THIS!"

I don't know how to log in!

There is no computer documentation on the face of the earth that tells you exactly what to do when you log in to your UNIX-based computer. That's why 99-44/100% of computer users gum up the edges of their monitors and keyboards with Post-it notes containing detailed step-by-step instructions.

Searching for Your Identity
(Easy as falling off a log(in)—NOT!!!!)

Once you have a login prompt on your screen, things get a lot easier. Oh, yeah!!

To use a UNIX system, you have to tell UNIX who you are, and then you have to type in a password to help prove that you're who you say you are. It's almost like the secret knock you made up for your secret club back when you were eight.

If you didn't set up your system, the person who did set it up—that person you were advised to get chummy with a few pages back—should have told you your login id and initial password. In fact, you may have had a chance to choose them yourself.

BUZZWORDS

LOGIN ID

Your *login id* (pronounced log-in-eye-dee) is publicly known—it's the name by which you are known in UNIXland—your "handle," for you old CB-ers out there. When people want to send you electronic mail, for instance, they address it using your UNIX login id along with the name of your system. More on this in Part 5.

People can look up your login id. Your *password*, on the other hand, must be kept private. It's the secret code that ensures that no one can log in pretending to be you, mess up your files, or send nasty electronic mail under your name. You learn how to change your password in a little bit; first you have to log in.

Logging In

The login prompt is UNIX's way of signaling that it's ready for you to log in and start working. The *cursor* immediately follows the login prompt.

BUZZWORDS

CURSOR

A cursor is a blinking (or not-blinking) dash or rectangle that appears on-screen to show you where the next thing you type will appear.

Alternative spelling: "curser"—when spelled this way, the term refers to the person working (or attempting to work) at the #@!!*&^ keyboard.

At the login prompt, type your login id (the public part) and press the Enter key. If your login id was "kitalong," for example, your first attempt might look like this:

```
login: kitalomg
```

What happens if you type the login id incorrectly, as poor ol' kitalong did in this example? Well, if you catch the mistake before you press the Enter key, you can erase it. How? One of several strategies ought to work.

Erasing things you didn't mean to type in UNIXland

✔ Use the Backspace or Delete key. If either of these works, you're lucky.

✔ Try the # key (press Shift-3). This works on some UNIX-based computers.

✔ Try the Ctrl-h key sequence—press and hold down the Control key (sometimes labeled Ctrl) and type the letter *h*. This is also known as the command from ...er... heck. That's because people immediately ask, "What the ...er, heck does typing an *h* have to do with erasing a mistake?" Just one of the many wonderfully intuitive things UNIX causes you to do against your will.

✔ If you aren't successful with any of these erasure techniques, just press the Enter key, type any old keys when UNIX asks for your password, press Enter one more time, and start all over.

Something to remember about UNIX: login ids and other commands are case-sensitive.

BUZZWORDS

CASE-SENSITIVE

Case-sensitivity, to UNIX, means that Kitalong and kitalong are two different login ids. In other words, UNIX interprets upper- and lowercase letters differently. Usually, login ids are all lowercase.

OK, once more with feeling.

```
login: kitalong
passwd:
```

Go ahead, type your password. Notice anything weird? Yes, nothing shows up on-screen. Your password is secret. So if anyone is in your office, looming over your shoulder as you work, they won't find out your password by reading it on-screen. However, they could watch where your fingers go on the keyboard, so beware if you're working with slimy or excessively nosy people!

What happens if you type something incorrectly during the two-step login process? UNIX helpfully tells you, `Login incorrect`.

"I HATE THIS!"

I don't know what I did wrong!

Unlike your mother, UNIX doesn't enumerate all your faults. It just says, "You did it wrong," and voila, you're back at the login prompt. It's up to you to figure out your own mistakes and try to avoid making the same ones next time.

Think of UNIX as your significant other: "If you loved me, you'd know what you did wrong!"

You might think it's excessive to spend so much time talking about all the mistakes one can make just logging in. It's a huge hurdle for EVERY-ONE! After you get used to it, it's as easy as falling off a log(in), but it takes a while to do it smoothly and suavely.

When you FINALLY type your login id and password correctly, you find yourself logged in. How do you know that? The clue is often a string of characters (which is usually the name of your machine) followed by a number in parentheses and then a percent sign. Here is an example:

```
professor(22)%
```

This is called the *UNIX prompt* or the *system prompt*. It signifies that UNIX is there—ready and waiting for you to tell it what to do. If your prompt doesn't look this one, don't worry. Prompts may look different for a variety of reasons, as explained later in this chapter. See Chapters 3 and 4 for more clues.

TIP

If, when you log in, your screen fills up with a bunch of squares and little pictures (trash basket, file cabinets, calendar, calculator), you're one of the lucky ones. Someone has set up a Graphical User Interface (GUI) for you! Now you can put off learning about UNIX for a while. Read Chapter 5 about graphical user interfaces.

Why does your machine have a name? Because it's probably connected to a network. Besides your login id and password, UNIX likes—actually NEEDS—to know which networked machine you are using. This is a rational need that you learn more about in Chapter 16.

In the sample login prompt shown previously, "professor" is the name of a UNIX machine used by faculty in a particular college department (not to be confused with the machine used by students, which is named "gilligan").

EXPERTS ONLY

Read this if you want to know why UNIX machines need names

In UNIXland, machines connected to the Internet are assigned unique numbers. No two machines on the Internet have the same identifying number. The names, like "professor" and "gilligan," or more dignified names like "psychology1" and "accounting," are supposed to make it easier for humans to remember their machine's name. The network and UNIX really prefer numbers. (See Chapters 16 and 17 for more on the Internet.)

I HATE UNIX!

✔ You're not running the System V version of UNIX. If that turns out to be the case, some other things in this book may not work either, but that doesn't necessarily mean you've wasted your money. Many things still work, because UNIX commands are standardized. See Chapter 3 for information on other versions of UNIX.

✔ Someone who knows what they're doing may have altered the appearance of your prompt. For instance, it's possible to program the prompt to display the pathname of the current directory, so you can keep track of where you are in UNIXland. (If you didn't understand that last statement, don't worry. It's explained in the next section.)

OK, what about the rest of the stuff in the UNIX prompt? Take another look at it:

```
professor(22)%
```

The number in parentheses is just the number of commands that have been executed during this logged-in session. That number may be higher than you think it should be, because it may include some commands that were issued behind the scenes as you logged in. The number changes each time you tell the computer to do something.

Finally, the percent sign is the UNIX prompt; see Chapter 3 for more on the different "flavors" of UNIX and how their prompts may differ from the one you see. For example, your prompt may end in a dollar sign ($) instead of a percent sign (%).

What good is the prompt? Well, it signifies to you that the computer is ready to accept your *input* (commands, directions). You notice the cursor, blandly blinking (or not-blinking) right after the prompt. That shows you where things appear when you start to type.

Exploring Your System (Using basic commands)

When you got a new bike for your eighth birthday, the first thing you wanted to do was try it. It should be the same with your first UNIX experience. Adopt that childlike abandon, and dig right in!

Home, James!

Your *home directory* is where you land when you first log in. It's a part of the computer disk that belongs only to you. It is where your files are stored (when you have some files).

BUZZWORDS

FILE

A *file* is a chunk of information that has been created and stored on a computer's disk. Almost anything can make up a file—a program, a letter, a collection of data.

The UNIX computer on which your files "live" has a relatively large storage device attached to it, called a *disk*. You can think of the disk as divided into sections, or *partitions*. Each person who is authorized to use the system gets a share of the disk's partitions in which to store files. Files reside in other sections of the disk that are necessary for running the computer.

I HATE UNIX!

BUZZWORDS

ACCOUNT

In UNIXland, *account* is shorthand for "a login id, password, and authorization to use the system's resources, like disk storage, memory, and CPU time." (Whew!) In other words, if you're an authorized user of a UNIX computer system, you have an account on that system.

Making a List, Checking It Twice

You may already have some files in your home directory. Perhaps the person who set up your computer placed some there. Or perhaps you have already been working on the system a bit. In any case, there's only one way to find out if you have files—try to list them with this command:

```
ls
```

"I HATE THIS!"

Nothing happened!

Oops—did you remember to press the Enter key after typing the command? Every time you type a command, you must register that command with the computer by pressing Enter. Pressing Enter tells the computer, "I'm done typing this command; now go to it!" Sometimes the key, which is usually located on the right side of your keyboard, is labeled Return or Send. In this book, it's always called the Enter key.

If you have files in your home directory, and you use the `ls` command, the names of the files are displayed on-screen, something like this:

```
documents   mail.data   report.4.glen   sales.data
```

If you didn't see anything—that is, if the UNIX % prompt just comes back without showing you anything, try the `ls` command with the all option. The syntax looks like this:

```
ls -a
```

Don't forget to put in a space between the *s* and the hyphen.

SYNTAX

Syntax is a general description of how a command is typed, what options are available, and what arguments the command accepts. For example, in the command **ls -a, ls** is the command, **a** is an option, and the argument is implied—UNIX understands that the argument is the current directory.

OPTION

An *option* is a modifier for a command that specfies in what way the command should be executed. In UNIXland, options are usually signalled by a hyphen (-).

ARGUMENT

Arguments are values or variables attached to a command. In the case of the **ls** command, **filename** is the argument, but it is often an implied argument, as explained earlier.

Now, you probably see some files whose names begin with a period, like this:

```
.cshrc        documents      report.4.glen
.login        mail.data      sales.data
```

Files that begin with a period are often *system files* that are required for UNIX and software to work.

CAUTION

> You should never, ever remove any system files, move them to another location, or even rename them. Chapter 7 explains how to move, remove, and rename files, but don't do any of those things to files beginning with a period (.).

Well, this is getting boring. If UNIX is such a powerful operating system, how come all we've done so far is log in and list files? Let's go on to something more fun.

Who Am I?

To find out who you are, see a psychiatrist, ask your parents, or type:

id

If you do the latter while your cursor is at a UNIX prompt, you see a response like the following:

```
uid=3687(kitalong) gid=101(hustud)
groups=101(hustud),10(staff)
```

UNIX lovers use this command a lot. For the rest of us, it's mainly a harmless command used to get us in the habit of typing things in UNIX.

Another harmless command is who, which tells you the identity of other people logged in to your system. (Try it, you'll like it!) You see something like this:

```
who
kitalong ttyp0    Nov 29 06:10              (trmsrv06.tc.mtu.)
```

In this example, only one person is logged in. Of course, it's only 6:10 a.m., as the Date/Time field of the command output tells us. Other things you can learn by reading this information: the person's login id (kitalong), the type of terminal (ttyp0), and the point at which the person accessed the network (trmsrv06.tc.mtu).

Where Am I?

Psychiatrists are supposed to help you find yourself. In UNIXland, the "find yourself" command is pwd, short for Print Working Directory (or, as a fellow UNIX-hater says, Print What Directory). Try it:

pwd

UNIX responds by printing the name of the current directory right on-screen (not on your printer). It looks something like this:

```
/usr/local/homes/kitalong
```

In this example, the working directory is still kitalong's home directory. We know that because kitalong is the right-most item in the path. The response you get to the pwd command looks quite different, especially if you have been experimenting with traveling-through-UNIXland commands. For example, your login id may not appear in the path name at all, or it may be buried somewhere in the middle. Traveling-through-UNIXland commands are introduced throughout this book. When you start exploring your UNIX system, pwd becomes an essential tool.

Passwords: The Key to System Security

Now that you've practiced typing a few commands, and have started to get your bearings in UNIXland, you need to take care of a critical responsibility—changing your password. Embed the following rules in your brain:

✔ Change your password immediately, and change it again about once a month for the rest of your natural life.

✔ Never, ever tell anyone your password.

These two rules are very important. They can't be stressed enough. Don't be insulted if these rules are repeated throughout this book.

When you first get an account on a UNIX-based system, your assigned password probably follows the same pattern as everyone else's. A common initial password is your Social Security number or your login id. These are not secret! Anyone can find out either.

Why the big secret?

✔ Changing your password frequently helps to protect your files and your colleagues' files from unauthorized use by coworkers and other passersby.

✔ Curious, mischievous, and sometimes malicious people, called *crackers* or *hackers*, make it their business to try to gain unauthorized access to as many computer systems as they can. Yours is no exception.

✔ If your computer system allows you to access wide-area networks like the Internet, your files are at risk. High-quality, secure passwords are the first line of defense against hackers.

BUZZWORDS

HACKER

Hackers are people who love computers so much that they use them OUTSIDE OF WORK HOURS. These sick people even love UNIX! As a hobby, they get a big charge out of using password-cracking programs to guess passwords; when they do this, they are sometimes called *crackers*. After one of these weirdos guesses your password, he or she can log in to your account. Sometimes they have malicious intent and sometimes they do so Just Because They Can.

How To Change Your Password

The command for changing your password is

```
passwd
```

After you enter this command, follow these steps:

1. You are prompted to type your current password. This is to protect you against slimy coworkers who might change your password when you're not looking. You should respond by typing the password you used when you first logged in today. Then press Enter.

2. You are asked to type a new password. What should you type? See the checklist for designing a creative, memorable, and ultra-secret password later in this section. Then type your new password and press Enter.

3. You are asked to type the same creative, memorable, and ultra-secret password again. This is to protect you from yourself. Two out of every three people mistype their password while changing it (they can't type their top-secret, ultra-creative, memorable password the same way twice). Also, every UNIX user has—at least once—forgotten his or her memorable password five seconds after typing it. Typing it twice is a hedge against that embarrassingly inevitable eventuality.

4. If you did everything right, you have a new password. UNIX says, `NIS entry changed on machine_name` (but substituting your machine's name for `machine_name`). The next time you log in, you have to use this password, exactly as you typed it. Don't forget it!

   If you did something wrong, UNIX says, `Incorrect password`, or something equally helpful. Start over and repeat these steps until you get it right!

The General Rule about Passwords: *A good password is one that is easy for you to remember, but difficult for someone else to guess.*

How to design a creative, memorable, and ultra-secret password

✔ In UNIXland, passwords are between four and eight characters long. Some systems are programmed to think that four characters are not enough. Some systems accept passwords longer than eight characters. Experiment with a variety of password formats to find out what your system tolerates.

✔ Remember, UNIX is case-sensitive. So your password can include both upper- and lowercase letters. It may also include numbers or special characters such as &_+=(<>).

✔ Random combinations of letters and numbers make excellent passwords, because they are virtually impossible to guess. However, you might find it virtually impossible to remember a password like 2B4g990q unless it means something to you!

✔ Make up a sentence, then create a password from the first (or last) letter of each word in the sentence. "Peas, potatoes, and pineapples are good for you" becomes Ppapagfy (or ssdsedru). If you want to get even trickier, use the number 4 in place of the f you got from the word "for." Ppapag4y makes a dynamite password!

✔ Use unusual capitalization in a relatively common word; how about something like DenIZeN?

✔ Misspell a relatively common word. A creative gardener, for example, might remove or change letters in the names of flowers, like this: hycinth. You can combine this tactic with some unusual capitalization, as in nAstrShM or dDdaiZy.

✔ Create nonsense words or combine short words in unusual ways, like clipFox or liBOPken. You can think up better ones than those!

✔ If you know a second language, use it along with some unusual capitalization. How about Finnish: vartija (watchman)? Or Belauan: ngarngii (we are)? Obviously, the more unusual the language, the better.

The Password Hall of Shame

Top 10 Easiest-to-Guess Passwords

10. Your dog's name

9. Your street name

8. Your phone number

7. Your significant other's name or phone number

6. The name of any member of your immediate family

5. Your car license plate

4. Your company name

3. 4- to 8-letter obscenities

2. Any word found in a dictionary

1. Any word found in a dictionary, spelled backward

If you work with slimy or nosy people, avoid passwords that commemorate your friends, relatives, lovers, pets, or other well-known things about you. If your computer is on a network, avoid dictionary words and obscenities. You are a sitting duck for a good guesser.

CAUTION

Password-cracking programs compare the passwords stored on a UNIX system with lists of words, such as dictionary entries, names, and acronyms. If your password matches one of the words in one of the lists, the program can decipher the password, even though it is encoded. Once the program has deciphered your password, it's a simple matter for a hacker or cracker to log in to your account, even if the machine that your account lives on is in Tallahassee and the hacker is in Paris.

BUZZWORDS

ENCODED

Encoded means scrambled. When you were in the fourth grade, you and your friends probably invented a secret code in which you assigned numbers or other letters to each letter of the alphabet in some special way. Password encoding works something like that, only, of course, it is much more complex. Sometimes, encoding is called *encrypting*.

One last cardinal rule: Never write your password anywhere! If you have to write it down to remember it, it's not a good password!

Forgotten Passwords

Everyone forgets their password at least once. When this happens to you, talk to your system administrator or the person who administers accounts on your system. That person cannot look up your password for you, because UNIX passwords are encoded before they are stored on the system. The system administrator (maybe that's you!) can change your password back to its initial state. Then it must be changed again. This time, make it something you remember!

Logging Out

If you've had enough and want to call it a day, it's very important that you log out, to keep the system secure. It's also very easy; at a UNIX prompt, type

>   logout

If `logout` doesn't work, try typing

>   exit

or

>   **Control-d** (press and hold the Ctrl key and press the letter *d*)

After you've pressed the Enter key, you should see the `login:` prompt on the screen, ready for the next time you want to work.

If you get a message such as `Not a login shell`, you are probably working in a shell window in a graphical user interface. You have to exit this environment before you can log out. See Chapter 5 for more on GUIs.

To help you remember your new password, you might want to log back in right away. You can then log out immediately without doing anything else.

CHAPTER 2
Getting Help

IN A NUTSHELL

▼ Ask the experts
▼ The man pages
▼ Other sources of help

Y ou may already have figured out that no one learns UNIX completely solo. This chapter describes ways to get help navigating in UNIXland.

Ask the Experts

Whether you have been working with UNIX for a day or a decade, there is always someone who knows more than you do. Expert users are the lifeblood of a UNIX-dependent organization. Ask around; find someone who knows UNIX, or at least, someone who likes it a little better than you do at this point. Cultivate that person's good graces. Think of them as your guru.

Disguises assumed by UNIX gurus

✔ Your system administrator.

✔ The person down the hall who always catches on to new technology before anyone else.

✔ The college kid who works at the deli across the street.

You can't tell where you'll find your guru, so keep your eyes and ears open.

When you ask a guru a question about a UNIX command, she immediately counters with a question of her own: "Did you check the man pages?"

The man Pages

The *man pages* are UNIX's idea of on-line help. Almost every version of UNIX comes with man pages, one for each UNIX command.

"I HATE THIS!"

Why are they called *man* pages and not *woman* pages?

Because man is short for manual. It's not an intentional affront to half of the world's population. It's just a command: man. If it really bugs you, learn the alias command and customize your system. Change the man command to woman, help, or any other word you choose. (See Chapter 18 if you want to try this.)

What man pages are not

- ✔ Sexist
- ✔ Macho
- ✔ A secret, computerized way for singles to find mates
- ✔ The opposite of woman pages

There are a lot of man pages! Some are very short (one or two screens), while others continue for 10 screens or more. To get to the man page for any command, type:

```
man command_name
```

substituting the command you want for *command_name*.

Why not take a look at the man page for the `ls` command, which was introduced in Chapter 1. Type:

man ls

Your screen should fill up with seemingly unintelligible words, as shown in this figure.

Part of the `ls` command's man page.

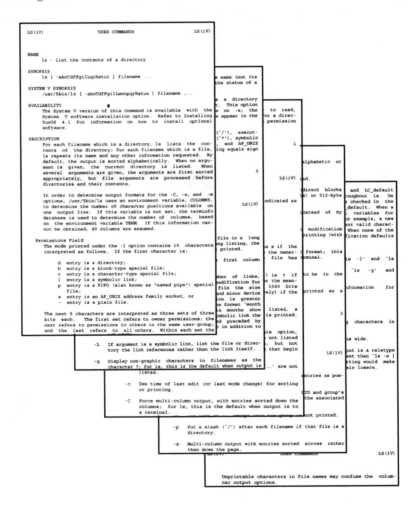

The tons of information provided by the man pages have good points and bad points:

What's bad: Man pages contain several different kinds of information, most of which you, a relative newcomer to UNIX, couldn't care less about.

What's good: The information is organized in a consistent way, so that once you are familiar with the organization and the content, you are able to skim for the information you need.

What information do man pages provide?

✔ *Name.* The command name and a short description of its use.

✔ *Synopsis.* Illustrates the command's syntax.

✔ *Description.* A long, agonizingly detailed description of how the command and its options work, how you enter the command's arguments, and, sometimes, what kind of response you can expect when you issue the command.

✔ *Files.* Lists all system files used or referred to by the command. This section is important to you if you program your own shell scripts.

✔ *See.* Provides a list of other man pages that contain information related to the command.

✔ *Diagnostics.* Explains how the command handles errors.

✔ *Bugs.* Warns you if the command has any known mistakes or limitations and how they are handled or circumvented.

Remember this neat-o dictionary game? You look up any word you don't know. Then, you look up the words you don't know in that word's definition. Here's how to adapt that egghead game to learning in UNIXland (think of it as self-education by way of the man pages):

1. Refer to the man page for any command.

2. Scroll down to the See section of the man page.

3. Memorize (or write down) the commands listed in the See section.

4. Exit the first man page and then type the man command for each of the commands you found in the See section.

5. Continue with the commands listed in the See section of each of the new commands.

6. Repeat until your eyes are bloodshot and your bottom is numb from sitting.

EXPERTS ONLY

The most-used parts of a man page

A man page is designed to be as complete and detailed a record of the command as possible. Therefore, you will neither understand nor care about most of the information you find in a man page, except for the Name, Syntax, and Description items.

Other Sources of Help

This book is designed to get you going with UNIX. Its primary purpose is to get you over the hump and using UNIX like a pro. Many people never need another source of help besides *I Hate UNIX*, the man pages, and a guru. If, however, you surpass the level of UNIX found in this book and you want to get more in-depth, the following checklist tells you how:

Checklist

✔ Camp out in the computer section of your favorite bookstore. A new UNIX book is published approximately every 86 minutes.

✔ Read the documentation that came with your computer. In some circles, reading computer documentation is considered chic and progressive! If you don't travel in those circles, camouflage the documentation inside a comic book.

✔ GUI users only: Read the documentation (both printed and on-line) that came with your GUI. Since GUI documentation consists of pictures of windows and icons, there is no need to camouflage it. Most of your friends will probably think it's a comic book.

✔ Use the resources available on the Internet. On-line discussions related to UNIX are found via the rn (readnews) command, which is explained in Chapter 17, along with other Internet research strategies.

CHAPTER 3

UNIX Concepts—Just Enough to Get Started

IN A NUTSHELL

▼ What is UNIX?
▼ Why use UNIX?
▼ UNIX Flavors All Taste
  Pretty Much the Same

I f you started at the beginning of this book intending to work your way through to the end, you may be ready to step back and take stock. You've explored UNIXland a bit: you've logged in and out, changed your password, and practiced a few commands.

This chapter is a little different from most of the rest of the book—you forego hands-on learning to get a handle on some of the ideas UNIX is built on. The hands-on stuff returns in the next chapter; for now, sit back and relax—you don't need a computer by your side for this chapter, so read it during your morning commute—unless, of course, you're driving!

What Is UNIX?
(UNIX's uniqueness)

The short answer is that UNIX is an operating system. If we let it go at that, there would be no *I Hate UNIX* book, and you would be left wondering, "What's the big deal?" This section helps you understand what there is to love about UNIX. It may not make you love UNIX any more, but it may help you understand what appeals to true UNIX-lovers.

BUZZWORDS

OPERATING SYSTEM

An *operating system* is a kind of software that manages a computer's activities and resources. It provides the base on which other software, such as word processing programs, are able to run. It controls the activities of your peripheral hardware, such as printers and modems. The operating system also makes it possible for you to issue commands like `ls` and `man`.

For a 25-year-old operating system, UNIX is very spry, and getting spryer. The following sections describe some of the characteristics that make UNIX unique.

Multitasking

A computer running the UNIX operating system can apparently execute more than one program at a time. Well, to you and me, it might look like they're all being executed at once, but in reality, the computer is programmed to rapidly "juggle" the programs or processes, devoting its attention to each in turn. Multitasking is sometimes called *multiprocessing*. But multiprocessing also has another, more specialized definition. To avoid unnecessary confusion, this book sticks to the term multitasking.

BUZZWORDS

PROCESSES

In UNIXland, *processes* are commands in the process of executing. Your login is a process. Any command that you issue is too, but only while it is executing. You learn a little more about processes in Chapter 18.

Multiuser

Multiuser means many terminals are connected to one UNIX-based computer and many users can log on at once. In fact, a user can log on from more than one terminal simultaneously. Each user works in his or her own individualized space, without interfering with anyone else's activities. This is particularly efficient because everyone on the system can share common data, without stepping on each other's toes.

Spooling

Multiuser and multitasking operating systems, of which UNIX is the best example, also enable each of those many users to use the same printer. If you and your coworker both have to print something at the same time, your jobs are *spooled* and printed in the order they are received.

Spooling is a real cost saver, because you no longer need a printer for every workstation. It also provides a diversion on the day before a long weekend. Why not organize the "Print Spooler Olympics," in which the owner of the print job that gets printed first is eligible for valuable prizes?

Programmable Shells

When you work with UNIX, you're not actually working *with* UNIX. You're working with a *shell*, also known as a *command interpreter*. It provides a buffer between you and the UNIX *kernel*.(No one talks directly to the kernel!!) If your computer is a workstation with a graphical user interface, you can open a window in which you type UNIX commands. (See Chapter 5 for more information on using UNIX with a GUI.) Technically, we should probably say "shell commands," instead of "UNIX commands," but let's not get picky.

You can write programs called *shell scripts* to help you do your job more efficiently. Some of the commands you learn in this book are actually shell scripts, but most of us never know the difference.

Shells come in three (or maybe four) flavors: The Bourne Shell (and its nephew the Bourne-again Shell); the Korn Shell (which is basically a beefed-up Bourne Shell, in about the same way that korn-fed cows are beefed-up for your dining pleasure); and the C Shell, which you can hold to your ear if you want to hear the ocean. (NOT!!!)

This book assumes—somewhat arbitrarily—that you are running a C Shell. Hence, the UNIX system prompt in all the examples ends with a % (percent sign). If you are running a Korn or a Bourne Shell, your prompt ends in a $ (dollar sign). The prompt is the only truly obvious difference among the shells, if you're a beginning UNIX user. Later on, when you get so good that people start looking you up when they have a question, you will probably develop an opinion about which shell is better and why. Until then, just play along.

Device Independence

The UNIX operating system runs on many different computers; another commonly used word for this is *portability*. To you, the end user, UNIX looks and acts about the same, regardless of which type of computer it's running on. In addition, if you design a word processor used on a UNIX-based Sun workstation, it is relatively easy to *port* (transport) that word processor to a Sequent computer running Dynix, Sequent's version of UNIX. In other words, Sun UNIX and Sequent UNIX are not different languages, but slightly different dialects of the same language.

32-Bit Processing

Machines that run UNIX usually house 32-bit *processors* (chips), rather than 8- or 16-bit chips. For practical purposes, a 32-bit chip makes a computer seem to run faster and lets it handle larger programs. Truthfully, most PCs made today use 32-bit chips, and the new Pentium chip that Intel makes is potentially a 64-bit chip.

How do you use this information? When you are shopping for a new computer, either for work or for home, surreptitiously check the specifications on the off-chance that some sleaze-ball would stoop so low as to try to sell you a machine with an 8- or 16-bit chip. (If there is such a

thing as a new computer with an 8- or 16-bit chip, it's been sitting in a warehouse for a long time.) Otherwise, forget you ever learned about processor speed and get on with your life.

EXPERTS ONLY

What good are chips chock full of bits?

✔ Chips with more bits can handle more data at a time.

✔ More data handling capability means that they can handle larger, more complex programs. (If you've ever tried to run Microsoft Windows on a 286 PC—which has a 16-bit chip—you can appreciate the importance of this.)

✔ The more bits at a time a chip can handle, the faster the chip (and the computer) are, although the speed doesn't go up proportionately with the size of the chip.

✔ Larger chips can handle more random-access memory, which, again, means added speed.

Why Use UNIX?

If speedy, efficient multiuser and multitasking capabilities don't impress you, maybe you should know the following facts.

Checklist

✔ Hundreds of vendors produce UNIX-based computer systems.

✔ Hundreds more offer software, hardware, and value-added services.

> ✔ UNIX has three key advantages—convenience, connectivity, and control—that keep it in the forefront of new computer purchases for large and small workgroups alike.

The next three sections discuss the three key advantages of using UNIX.

UNIX Is Convenient

Especially because of UNIX's speed and multiuser, multitasking capability, it's a very efficient computing environment. Several users at once can share common data and other files stored on a central machine. When one person makes updates to the payroll system, for example, those updates are automatically available to everyone who needs them.

UNIX Means Connectivity

Most UNIX installations are networked, or will be eventually.

BUZZWORDS

NETWORK

Basically, a *network* is a bunch of computers usually connected with wires, although wireless networks are beginning to appear.

As you will see in Chapters 15, 16, and 17, UNIX's networking capabilities link you with a vast array of resources and people, both locally and internationally, who can enrich your life and extend your peer group beyond your customary geographical confines.

I HATE UNIX!

HUH?

BUZZWORDS

LANs and WANs

A LAN (*local-area network*) connects computers in the same company, building, or section of a building. The main reason for a local-area network is to share files and printers. A WAN (*wide-area network*), on the other hand, connects computers that are geographically separated. Such networks feature electronic mail, remote login, and file transfer programs. The Internet is the largest WAN. It is usually described as a vast international "network of networks" that connects educational institutions, government agencies, and businesses in a giant web. More on the Internet in Chapters 16 and 17.

UNIX Gives You Control—When You Want It

Many people do a lot of work with UNIX without ever learning it. Wherever UNIX-based computers are installed, you find people who know little or nothing about the underlying UNIX operating system who, nonetheless, use spreadsheets, electronic mail, drafting packages, and word processing programs. It's possible to go on for a long time this way, but users lose some measure of control if they never learn what makes UNIX tick. When they are ready to learn, though, UNIX is there; and barring some minor updates and superficial system-to-system differences, UNIX is likely to stay stable.

I HATE UNIX!

EXPERTS ONLY

What happened to DOS?

✔ You need not pretend that you never heard of DOS; it's not outré—in fact, it's still very much alive and well on personal computers. DOS, after all, was based on UNIX, so some of the commands are similar, although UNIX boasts many more features, commands, variations, and options than DOS does.

✔ If you try UNIX for a while and find that you keep typing the DOS variant of the command you want to execute, welcome to the club. People do get attached to operating systems, and are loath to relinquish the known territory of DOSville for the unknown and perhaps dangerous UNIXland. You will jump for joy when you learn the UNIX alias command in Chapter 18. It lets you rename UNIX commands, like **ls**, to something you can live with, like DIR.

Cliff Notes Version of the History of UNIX (39 flavors of UNIX? No, only two)

UNIX was born at Bell Labs in the 1960s, and remained largely cloistered within the Bell system until the mid-1970s. Bell (or AT&T, if you like) generously licensed its UNIX v-e-r-y cheaply to educational institutions. Although legend has it that AT&T gave UNIX away because it was prohibited from selling it, this is a good place to start a new rumor. Let's all spread the word that AT&T/Bell invented that now age-old computer vendor trick of giving stuff to schools in hopes that kids and teachers become hooked on their technology. We all know the purpose of that strategy—it leads parents and corporations to buy the technology those spoiled school kids are accustomed to using, thereby ensuring the vendors continued profitability. Capitalism at its best.

Anyhow, to make a short story long, the University of California at Berkeley refrained from looking a gift horse in the mouth. They glommed on to AT&T UNIX and developed it to the point where they ended up with their own version of UNIX, which they creatively named Berkeley UNIX, a.k.a. BSD UNIX. (BSD stands for Berkeley Software Distribution.)

Meanwhile, AT&T continued its own development of UNIX, which resulted in the introduction of System V UNIX in the early 1980s, surpassing Systems I through III (but inexplicably skipping IV). For about 10 years, these two strains of UNIX —Berkeley and System V—proliferated in parallel formation. With the publication of formal standards developed over this 10- or 12-year period, a blended flavor of UNIX has finally emerged.

UNIX System V, Release 4.2 (SVR4.2), the UNIX release covered in this book, is expected to go forward as THE UNIX STANDARD for the end of the century. This is good news for those of us who don't care what command we have to type, as long as we don't have to remember which UNIX is which!

But every silver lining has a cloud. The bad news is that your computer may not be running SVR4.2 yet. That means that some things in this book may not work.

TIP

If things do not work as we say they should in this book, do not automatically assume that you are at fault. It might be that specific commands are different on your release of UNIX. This is common. Do not, we repeat, *do not* assume that you are stupid if this happens.

When you learn the correct command for your system, write it on a Post-it note and stick it on your monitor or on the relevant page in the book. You can even write it directly in the book, if it's your personal copy.

How can you find out what version of UNIX you are running? The next time you log in, check all that garbage that flashes on the screen before the prompt comes up. Somewhere in that batch of messages is a statement about your computer's flavor of UNIX. It's not a bad idea to try to remember that little piece of information, just in case you want to impress someone.

EXPERTS ONLY

Asking UNIX its name
If you want to find out for sure what version of UNIX is running on your system, try typing

`uname`

at the UNIX prompt.

"I HATE THIS!"

You say to-may-to, I say to-mah-to
The two main versions of UNIX have leeettttle, niggling differences. For example, one of them likes the print command `lp`, while the other likes `lpr`. It's kinda arbitrary. Can't we all just get along?

CHAPTER 4

The Care and Feeding of UNIX Hardware Setups

IN A NUTSHELL

- ▼ Identifying your hardware setup
- ▼ Single-user systems
- ▼ Multiuser systems
- ▼ The system administrator

Y ou might have gathered from reading Chapter 1 that sometimes UNIX runs on a multiuser system and sometimes on a single-user system. Back in Chapter 1, you also learned about the perils of turning your UNIX system on and off, especially if your desktop computer is a workstation. In this chapter, you learn just a little bit more about hardware, about how it can peacefully coexist with the UNIX in your life, and about the "wetware" (brain power) you need to help keep all this hardware running.

Identifying Your Hardware Setup (Just a reminder)

In Chapter 1, you learned that there are three ways you can access a multiuser UNIX setup.

Types of hardware access to multiuser UNIX
✔ Workstation
✔ Terminal
✔ PC acting as terminal

You also learned that your workstation should NEVER be turned off, because it may be connected to a network on which it performs a crucial function for other people. You learned, too, that terminals and PCs can be turned off once you have issued the `logout` command or otherwise exited gracefully from UNIXland.

This chapter complicates things just a tiny bit more by talking in a little more depth about single-user and multiuser UNIX systems.

Single-User Systems

PCs and Macs that have a version of UNIX installed right on their hard disk can often function as single-user systems. If you bought AUX for your Macintosh, for example, you are probably running UNIX in single-user mode. (AUX is the Macintosh version of UNIX.)

What UNIX for a PC buys you

✔ You can prove your love for UNIX by working in the UNIX environment all the time.

✔ You can run software designed for personal computers running UNIX.

✔ You can take full advantage of UNIX's multitasking ability. In other words, you can do many things at once (as if you don't already).

If you've purchased UNIX for your PC, a book must have been included. Read it. You can probably learn lots of useful things, such as how commands work, and how to turn your system on and off without breaking anything. Most likely, there is a special command (perhaps `shutdown`) that enables you to exit gracefully from UNIXland.

I HATE UNIX!

Multiuser Systems

Most UNIX systems are designed to accommodate more than one user at a time. In this book, we assume that you are working on a multiuser system running UNIX System V Release 4.2 and the C Shell. Depending on who you talk to, this may or may not be a valid assumption; as you learned in an earlier chapter, every UNIX lover has an opinion about which is the best, most common, or most versatile shell!

This book also assumes that you are not—at least not *solely*—responsible for managing the system. If you are solely responsible for managing the system—that is, if you are the system administrator, or sys-ad for short—and this book is your first exposure to UNIX, you need to get another book, go to sys-ad school, or find another job.

Multiuser UNIX systems are sometimes operated in single-user mode. If the system administrator has to do some work on the system, he or she must sometimes throw everybody out and switch to single-user mode to get the work done. (Remember how your mom or dad threw you out of the kitchen during holiday meal preparations? Same thing.)

HUH?

BUZZWORDS

MODE

When programs can operate in more than one specific way, each way is called a *mode*. For example, a spreadsheet I work with allows me to run in regular mode when I'm entering and manipulating data, but I can switch to graphics mode if I want to see exactly how the page will look when I print it. Likewise, multiuser UNIX setups can be operated in single-user mode when necessary.

Anyway, it should be obvious whether you're using a single-user or multiuser system. If you're the only one who works at this company, odds are it's a single-user UNIX system. If you and a bunch of other people are connected to a central computer, either within the building or off-site somewhere, then it's a multiuser system.

The System Administrator (Your friend and mine)

The *system administrator* is the technical person in charge of keeping the computers running. As a rule, system administrators are to be obeyed. Some of them have poor communication skills, but they are smart, good-hearted, and concerned, above all, with the proper functioning of your computer system.

How to choose a system administrator

✔ *Best Method:* Hire or train a designated system administrator.

✔ *OK Method:* Convince people already on your staff to—either willingly or not—assume the system administrator job.

✔ *Another OK Method:* Contract with a vendor or another person outside of the company to be an on-call system administrator.

✔ *Bad Method:* Take a vote while somebody is out of the room, and elect him or her to be system administrator.

If you are running a single-user UNIX system, you are the system administrator. That's OK. Even if you don't know what you're doing at first, your screwups won't make hash out of anyone else's files but your own.

On a multiuser UNIX system, single-user mode occurs when the system administrator decides that he or she has to fix something. What happens next?

1. The system administrator sends a message (probably electronically over the system) to all users, asking them to log out. The message might be something along the lines of, "Please log out, I have to fix something right now!!!" Or maybe, "Get out, I'm taking over!"

2. When everyone has had a chance to log out, the system administrator issues a command to switch the system to single-user mode, with him or her as the sole user.

3. The system administrator fixes the problem.

4. When the problem is fixed, or a determination made that it can't be fixed right now, the system administrator makes it known that everyone else may log back in. This time, an electronic message won't work, because everyone is logged out. The system administrator has to use a different method to clue everyone in.

Top 10 Methods of Telling Everybody to Log Back In

10. Write the message on a paper airplane and fly it to everyone.

9. Insert the message into a bottle and float it to everyone.

8. Announce it on the billboard across the street.

7. Call the radio station and have it put on the Community Calendar.

6. Shout, OK, guys, you can log back in now!

5. Announce it on the PA system.

4. Activate the phone tree, like the one the PTA uses—the sys-ad calls two people, who each call two people, and so on until everyone knows.

3. Put it in the company newsletter.

2. Tell the office informer.

1. Run around from office to office telling everyone.

Perhaps the easiest method is to turn the system back on at a predetermined time that everyone is aware of because it was in the original electronic message.

More than likely, the system administrator performs maintenance tasks that require system shutdown at weird hours—early in the morning, late at night, on weekends—when no one else is around because they are sleeping, pretending to sleep, or having fun. In fact, your system administrator may schedule a special day (or night) of the week for maintenance work to avoid disrupting the rest of the world.

In short, system administrators do not relish forcing a multiuser system into single-user mode, thereby disturbing you and the rest of your coworkers. So don't take it personally when your techie person says, perhaps rather tersely, that you must log out immediately. Just do it.

CHAPTER 5

Graphical User Interfaces

Or, a GUI Picture Is Worth a Thousand Words of UNIX

IN A NUTSHELL

▼ Do you have a GUI?
▼ UNIX and GUIs
▼ Types of GUIs
▼ Getting your own GUI

I HATE UNIX!

A GUI (pronounced "gooey") is a setup that allows you to communicate with UNIX by manipulating graphics with a mouse, instead of by typing commands. It takes over your screen, filling it up with little pictures, called *icons*, that represent programs running on your computer, and it divides your screen into areas called *windows*, in each of which you can do something different.

How to tell if you have a GUI

✔ When you log in, do you just see a single, boring UNIX prompt? You might have a GUI, but it's not activated yet. Read on.

✔ Do you have a mouse attached to your computer? That's a good sign—a mouse is needed to work with a GUI.

✔ Does your screen fill up with little pictures, boxes, and other neat-o things? That's a GUI! You're in business!

BUZZWORDS

MOUSE

A *mouse* is a little, sort of rectangular contraption that fits in your hand and is connected to the computer by means of a wire. When you set the mouse on your desk (preferably on a special pad made just for it) and you move it around, a little square or arrow or some other indicator called the *mouse pointer* moves around on your screen. When you press one of the buttons on the mouse while the pointer is pointing at something, you can make things happen on your screen!

Gotta Get a GUI

A GUI is a handy thing to have. If you don't see one on your screen, you should find out whether you can get one, and if so, how to get it. Try these steps:

1. Maybe you already have one—ask someone who knows if there's a command you can type to make a GUI come up on-screen.

2. Find out from someone who knows whether or not it's even possible for you to have one.

UNIX GUIs work best on workstations and other computers for which the operating system is UNIX (like a Macintosh running AUX). If you have a dumb terminal or a PC that acts like a dumb terminal, odds are that you won't be able to use a GUI, with the possible exception of X Windows.

3. Buy one and install it…or, better yet, get your company to buy it and your friend the sys-ad to install it for you.

How Can a GUI Simplify Your Life?

Here's an example of how a GUI can make life easier for you. Suppose you want to know which files are in your home directory. You already learned the command for this in Chapter 1—remember? It's ls. When you type ls at a UNIX prompt, you see something like this:

```
documents   mail.data   report.4.glen   sales.data
```

It's adequate, of course, but far from exciting. If you have a GUI, though, you have a file manager, which gives you a visual representation of the files in your home directory. In the Open Windows GUI, for example, the equivalent of the `ls` command would give you this:

The Open Windows GUI does `ls`.

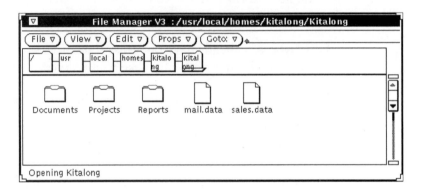

Isn't that a lot more exciting?

For more info on the popular UNIX GUIs, read on.

Why Learn UNIX in a Point-and-Click World?

Serious artists study human anatomy to improve their technical skill and help them understand what muscles and bones can do. Likewise, serious GUI users want to know something about UNIX, the bones and muscles that underlie their GUI, to help them understand what's happening when they point, click, and drag with their mouse. Now, you probably don't think of yourself as a serious computer user (after all, you are reading this book). But when you complement your growing knowledge of bare-bones UNIX with a graphical user interface, which is much more than just a pretty face, you're getting into some fairly serious technical-skill-improvement strategies. You might find yourself liking computers, if you're not careful.

UNIX and the GUI—A Powerful Team

If you've been reading straight through from the beginning of this book, you know that UNIX is an ancient operating system, dating back to the 1960s. It's been worked over continuously during all this time, by people who love it and want it to be all it can be. Consequently, UNIX commands or shell scripts are available—or can be written—to do anything that you could possibly think of doing. Well, anything on a computer, that is.

UNIX lovers think that UNIX's awe-inspiring physical prowess is just wonderful. But for mere mortals like us, facing such superhuman capabilities is a little frustrating—dare we say "intimidating?"

"I HATE THIS!"

I can't remember the @#$%^ command!

The problem with bare bones UNIX is that you have to remember which command does what. If you can't find a command that does what you have to have done, you have to combine a bunch of commands into a shell script that does the task you want to accomplish. Then, you have to type the commands precisely, because UNIX won't try to guess what you meant to type. You also have to know what to do with the output that results from the command you typed or the script you executed. This is all well and good, and it works just fine, but what if you're not good at remembering commands, or don't want to do any shell programming, or can't type worth beans?

If you have a GUI, all you have to do is manipulate a mouse to point, click, and drag in such a way as to activate programs, move stuff around, throw stuff away, and retrieve stuff that you have accidentally thrown away.

If you play a lot of Nintendo, this is a snap. If you aren't a product of the arcade generation, but are rather a member of the arcane generation, you might have some trouble. Your limited hand-eye coordination notwithstanding, GUIs are in, and you ought to be trying to figure out how you can score one for your computer.

Well, are you convinced? If you don't already have a GUI, how do you go about choosing one? For that matter, what choices are available?

Kinds of GUIs

You can get a GUI for your PC (Microsoft Windows is the most likely to succeed for DOS machines). Your Macintosh can't function without its GUI; it comes fully dressed and can't get nekkid, even for a system programmer. There are at least three GUIs vying for popularity in the UNIX arena.

The X Window System

For many UNIX users, X hits the spot. The X Window System (X for short) is probably the most widely used UNIX GUI, most likely because it's so readily available.

EXPERTS ONLY

You can even get X for free from MIT, if you're willing to spend some time customizing it for your particular hardware setup. Warning: Customizing X may sound like an eXcellent adventure, but only eXperts should take on the challenge. If you get to be an eXpert and want to try customizing your own X installation, you should be able to obtain the software from an anonymous FTP site on the Internet. See Chapters 16 and 17 for a full eXplanation.

Anyway, X is ultra-cool for two main reasons—well, three, if you count that fact that it can be obtained for free, but that's a miXed blessing.

Why is X cool?

✔ It can be made to work on most computers, even if they don't run UNIX.

Some people say, "It works on all computers," but I can't bring myself to be that sure. I know that the sky is up, and I know that my computer is sometimes down—those things I'm sure of. But if the subject of a sentence is the name of a computer or a software package, and the verb is "works," I always stick in a little element of doubt.

✔ If the computer you're using is on a network (see Chapters 15 through 17 for more on networks), the stuff you see on-screen can be housed on another computer. This is the feature that helps X (possibly) run on computers that aren't UNIX based. It also saves on costs in the form of disk storage space, memory needs, and network access times.

Motif and Open Look

Another reason you might think X is cool is because programmers don't have to follow specific standards of appearance and functioning for the programs they write for use with X. That means that people who design programs for the X Window System can be creative about how they place things in the GUI, how they make things look, and how functions are performed. Although variety may be the spice of life, this nod to the creative spirit may not be good for the end user. A peek at the Motif and Open Look systems' standards may help you understand why.

The Motif windowing system and the Open Look windowing system (of which Open Windows, mentioned earlier, is an implementation) strictly enforce the rule that programmers who want to create for their environments must develop products with a consistent "look and feel." This rule has the effect of stifling programmer creativity, but it is good for you, the user, because all programs you see in your GUI will look alike. The menus will be similar, and commands that perform similar functions will have similar names and will be found within the same menu items. Because of that built-in similarity, once you have learned one program, you'll be able to easily learn other programs and to switch between programs, so you'll spend less time making the transition from one program to the next.

So Ya Wanna Get a GUI, Eh?

Before you start whining for a GUI, do some research. Although you might not find anything as good as *Consumer Reports* for the computer industry, computer journals regularly include articles and advertisements about GUIs. Internet discussion groups are another good place to ask questions. You might want to use research to identify your first and second choices, and then ask questions like the following.

Things to ask when you go window shopping

✔ Is this a Motif, Open Look, or X-based GUI?

✔ How much does it cost?

✔ How much does it cost for use on the number of computers installed in your company?

✔ Can I test drive it?

✔ Can I test drive it on my own computer system?

✔ Will you speak with my system administrator?

When you've done your homework, you'll have to involve your system administrator in the final decision. Now, keep in mind that your system administrator undoubtedly has an opinion about GUIs. That opinion may consist of "Bah, humbug!" since system administrators don't always appreciate having to manipulate stupid little pictures to get their work done.

After the initial shock has worn off, however, the system administrator has a knack for coming up with a plethora of useful questions to ask the vendor—questions you never would have thought up in a million years!

Top 10 Things Sys-ads Like To Ask About GUIs

10. How much network bandwidth does this puppy suck up?

9. How much disk space does this puppy suck up?

8. How is this puppy licensed?

7. Will I be tied up with maintenance problems, fixing some stupid new quirk every day?

6. If something breaks, will the company fix it right away, for free?

5. Whose feet do I have to kiss to get technical support?

continues

Top 10 Things Sys-ads Like To Ask About GUIs (continued)

4. Do your technical support hotline people answer their voice mail, or do they ignore it like most hotline workers do?

3. Do you have this in stock or do I have to wait a year to get it?

2. Does this work on *insert brand name* computers?

1. Can you give me the names of some other fools… er, companies who have purchased this piece of trash from you?

In short, don't go GUI shopping without your system administrator. And, finally, don't expect to go to Computers R Us today and come home with a GUI. GUIs are like other major purchases; you may buy the first one you look at, but it's a good idea to look at others, just to make sure you're choosing wisely.

PART II

Making UNIX Do What You Want It To Do

Includes:

CHAPTER 6

Speaking UNIX
(and Getting What You Want)

IN A NUTSHELL

▼ Commanding so UNIX understands

▼ Interpreting UNIX responses

▼ Practice speaking UNIX

You are in charge when it comes to UNIX. But the caveat is that you've got to learn the commands and how to express them so that UNIX gets the drift and makes your every wish its command. This chapter is your introduction to UNIX command syntax—designed to release your inner Aladdin and turn UNIX into the magic genie. This chapter also prepares you for a little quirk of UNIX's—its relative silence after a command has been completed.

Commanding So UNIX Will Understand

In your brief acquaintance with UNIX, you've undoubtedly noticed that its command structure is a little weird.

Weird things about UNIX commands

✔ A lot of times they're only two letters long; a three-letter command is extravagant for UNIX. But, on the other hand, some commands are a whole word long. There's no consistency.

✔ There's no way to know which letters UNIX picks up on. For two-letter commands, it would be nice if UNIX always used either the first two letters of a command's full name, or the first letters of the words in the command. Instead, it's a real mishmash: `ls` for list, `cd` for change directory, `lp` for print (actually, line printer).

✔ Lots of times, the commands make no sense to ordinary people; for example, `cat` is the command for "print this file on the screen so I can take a look at it." What does a cat have to do with this objective? Nothing, unless you know that in UNIXland, *cat* stands for *concatenate* or *catenate*! Who knows words like that?!

✔ UNIX commands come equipped with a multitude of options that add functionality I'd never think of needing. What's the point?

✔ When I issue a UNIX command, most of the time UNIX simply completes the command without telling me, unless something goes wrong. It's downright creepy.

Command Syntax

UNIX commands, despite their apparent loathsomeness, are actually fairly predictable, at least as far as their syntax is concerned.

BUZZWORDS

SYNTAX

Contrary to popular belief, syntax is not a surcharge on sex, drugs, and rock and roll. Syntax refers to a set of rules that govern how symbols can be put together, either in a normal human language or in a computer language. You can think of it as "grammar." Just as English language syntax keeps you from saying "Ball the red is," so UNIX command syntax governs the order in which you can assemble elements of a command.

In general, UNIX commands follow this syntax, or pattern:

```
command [-option(s)] [argument(s)]
```

What the parts of a command mean

✔ `command` answers the question, "Do what?"

✔ `-` tells UNIX to expect one or more options

✔ `options` tell UNIX how the command should be executed

✔ `arguments` specify on what the command is operating

✔ `options` and `arguments` are bracketed in the example. When you see brackets in syntax, this means that the bracketed options and arguments aren't required for a command to do something. (Most commands do *something*, even without the bracketed elements.) When you type the actual command, DON'T include the brackets.

Here's how the command syntax works. You've already learned that you can list the files in your home directory by typing:

```
ls
```

`ls` is a command. Adding an option—say, to get a *long* list, or a list of *all* files including the hidden ones—involves adding a hyphen followed by the option's code. Often the code for an option reflects the name of the option in some way, but this is not necessarily the case.

To get a long (detailed) list of files in the current directory, you use the `ls` command with the `l` option. It looks like this:

```
ls -l
```

Here's an example of the output of this command:

```
total 4
drwxr-xr-x 2 kitalong  512 Nov 10  14:22  Documents
-rw-r--r-- 1 kitalong  272 Nov 18   8:05  mail.data
-rw-r--r-- 1 kitalong  536 Dec  5  19:02  report.4.glen
-rw-r--r-- 1 kitalong  138 Dec 14  14:53  sales.data
```

To get a list of all files in the current directory, type

ls -a

The output looks something like this:

```
.                 .login        report.4.glen
..                Documents     sales.data
.cshrc            mail.data
```

Combining options is easy; for example, to get a long list of all files, simply call for both options at once. Putting a minus sign in front of each option isn't necessary; you just string the options together like this:

```
ls -la
```

or

```
ls -al
```

TIP

> The order of the options usually doesn't matter. If it does, the man page tells you.

OK, now let's add the argument. To list all the files in a directory named Documents, using the long list format, type:

ls -la Documents

Here's what the command output would look like:

```
total 3
drwxr-xr-x  2  kitalong    512    Dec 15   14:18    .
drwxr-xr-x  2  kitalong    512    Dec 15   14:20    ..
-rw-r--r--  1  kitalong   1412    Dec 18   11:05    board.report
-rw-r--r--  1  kitalong   1412    Dec 16   10:22    report.4.char
-rw-r--r--  1  kitalong   1412    Mar 22   18:08    report.q1
-rw-r--r--  1  kitalong   1412    Dec 30   17:10    report.q4
```

Huh? Interpreting the Feedback You Get from UNIX

The output of the `ls` command is pretty straightforward. At least you can see on-screen what the command has done, even if you don't understand all of the gibberish it produces.

You may notice, however, that UNIX gives you no information other than exactly what you asked for. In other words, there are no frills, such as a label or title; all you get is the unadorned command results. In contrast, the DOS directory listing command, DIR, tells you the name of the disk it is listing for you and echoes back the directory command you issued, like this:

```
Volume in drive C is HARDDISK
Directory of  C:\

COMMAND   COM    25307    3-17-87   12:00p
WP51           <DIR>     10-24-93    7:26p
PBRUSH         <DIR>     10-24-93    8:33p
HATEUNIX       <DIR>     10-26-93    5:44a
CORRESP        <DIR>     11-20-93    8:59a
KERMIT         <DIR>     10-24-93    7:20p
WORD5          <DIR>     10-24-93    8:13p
```

```
MOUSE    SYS     15034   10-23-89   12:00p
CONFIG   SYS        87   10-24-93    8:26p
AUTOEXEC BAT        99   10-24-93    8:39p
JIM             <DIR>     1-01-80   12:55a
SYS      COM      4766    3-17-87   12:00p
DOS             <DIR>    10-24-93    6:42p
          13 File(s)  21893120 bytes free
```

"I HATE THIS!"

Why does UNIX have to be so close-mouthed?

UNIX programmers give a good reason for UNIX's taciturn behavior. They say that UNIX command output is often piped to the input of another command or redirected to a file. Just as a simple example, you can redirect the output of the ls command to a file named ListTest, like this:

```
ls > ListTest
```

Eliminating the "excess baggage" of labels, titles, and other niceties makes the programmers' job go more smoothly, because they don't have to strip out anything before executing the command. For mere mortals—like the rest of us who use UNIX only under duress—it is a royal pain.

UNIX gives you what you asked for without saying anything extra. Therefore, when you issue a command like mkdir, which makes a new subdirectory inside the current directory, UNIX just does it without saying anything. Once the prompt is back, there is no reason to think UNIX failed in its mission.

However, if there is a problem, UNIX usually tells you. Just like a bad boss, UNIX gives you feedback only when you've done something wrong.

Let's use the `mkdir` command as an example. Suppose you created a directory called Projects in your home directory, by issuing the command

```
mkdir Projects
```

Then suppose that you forgot you had created the Projects directory and tried to create it again. After you issued the `mkdir Projects` command, UNIX is quick to rub it in, by saying something like

```
mkdir: Projects: File exists
```

Actually, that's the C Shell talking. The response might be slightly different if you use the Korn or Bourne shell.

So UNIX sometimes gives you a warning, especially when it can catch you in the act of doing something foolish. In this case, you apparently were trying to replace an existing directory with a new directory of the same name. This would be destructive, and you might live to regret it. So UNIX (or the shell) calls your attention to it. In the same spirit, if you try to remove a directory that still has files inside it, using the `rmdir` command, UNIX refuses, saying

```
rmdir: Projects: Directory not empty
```

UNIX also makes a comment if it can't find the argument you are trying to issue a command on. For example, if you try to `cd` to a directory but mistype the directory name, UNIX expresses its confusion:

You: `cd Projetcs`
UNIX: `Projetcs: No such file or directory`

"I HATE THIS!"

> ### Why can't UNIX be just a little bit consistent?
> Yes, you read it correctly. When UNIX commented on the incorrect `mkdir` command, it repeated both the command and the argument. When it commented on the incorrect `cd` command, however, it repeated only the argument, not the command. Why are you surprised?

One more example. In the next chapter, you learn about the `rm` command, which lets you get rid of (remove) files. UNIX has a nasty habit of simply obeying, without protest, when you tell it to remove files. You have to specify "interactive" mode, with the `i` option (or have your system administrator do so globally, for everyone on the system), if you want UNIX to force you to verify the `rm` command.

The moral of the story is that UNIX often does its job silently, assuming that you know what you're talking about. You need to learn to live with that annoying little quirk in UNIX; sometimes it takes some customization, which you learn a little more about in Chapter 18.

Cute and Fun Commands To Help You Practice Speaking UNIX

UNIX isn't all admonitions and silent executions, though. If you try hard enough, you can find commands to have fun with.

News

Your system administrator might have implemented the news command as a way of making announcements to everyone who uses the system. To check, type:

news

at your system prompt. Pertinent announcements appear on-screen, if the command is working at your site. Getting into the habit of reading the news every day is a good idea. If, for example, your system administrator schedules some "down time" to work on the system, you will know about it in advance. Some companies also post other computer-related announcements, such as training programs, newly available software, and system backup times, as well as non-computer-related items such as cars for sale, apartments for rent, and company picnics.

Planning Ahead for the New Century

Try the cal command. It prints on-screen a little calendar of the current month, like this:

```
      December 1993
   S  M Tu  W Th  F  S
               1  2  3  4
   5  6  7  8  9 10 11
  12 13 14 15 16 17 18
  19 20 21 22 23 24 25
  26 27 28 29 30 31
```

Want to see what day your birthday is on in 1999? You can do it with

```
cal month year
```

If your birthday is in June, for example, the command looks like this:

```
cal 6 1999
```

You must type the entire year, because UNIX knows all the dates starting with the year 1 and continuing through 9999. If you just type `cal 6 99`, UNIX displays the month of June in the year 99!

Here's what June 1999 looks like:

```
    June 1999
 S  M Tu  W Th  F  S
          1  2  3  4  5
 6  7  8  9 10 11 12
13 14 15 16 17 18 19
20 21 22 23 24 25 26
27 28 29 30
```

To plan your schedule for the entire last year of the 1900s, use the `cal 1999` command without specifying a month:

```
cal 1999
```

Let's see, New Year's Eve falls on a Friday in 1999—do you think they'll give us the whole week off to celebrate?

CHAPTER 7

Directing Your Directories

IN A NUTSHELL

- ▼ Understanding directories and files
- ▼ Moving around in UNIX
- ▼ Creating and organizing directories
- ▼ Removing files and directories

You learned earlier in this book that any operating system, even UNIX, lets you control the information you create and store. You tell UNIX what to do. If UNIX understands your command, it obeys it. It's as simple as that.

In this chapter, you put UNIX to work for you managing the information on your UNIX account. In the brief time you've been fiddling around with UNIX, you already may have created some files with your word processing program or spreadsheet. In this chapter, you learn how to get these data-ducks in a row, march them all to the same drummer, and get rid of them when they're no longer needed. First, you have to understand what kind of organizational scheme UNIX uses.

Understanding UNIX Directories and Files

Are you ready for some jargon? Here goes: Information is stored hierarchically on a UNIX system. What does that mean?

BUZZWORDS

HIERARCHICAL FILE SYSTEM

In the real world, hierarchies are common. At work, for example, you probably have experience with an organizational chart that places the president at the top of the hierarchy, vice-presidents reporting to the president, and several managers reporting to each vice-president. The hierarchy assumes a pyramid shape—the top is very narrow and pointy, while the bottom is wide, because it includes many people. Hierarchical file systems operate on the same principle.

The most common analogy compares a hierarchical file system to an upside-down tree. In our universe, trees usually have their roots at the bottom, and their branches and leaves extending skyward.

However, in the UNIX universe (and in the DOS universe, too, for that matter), the *root* of the directory *tree* is conceptually at the top. All other entities in the system (branches, twigs, leaves, fruit) are conceptually "below" the root.

If the idea of an upside-down tree gives you the willies, another good way to imagine UNIX's root directory is as a huge file drawer. In this analogy, all the related entities are nested within it, rather than branched off of it.

File drawers are for organizing stuff. You know this, because you probably receive lots of paper in a given week. During a busy week, when you just throw all of that paper into a pile, even if you hide that pile inside a file drawer, you end up with a minor disaster—bowling banquet invitations jumbled together with invoices, cartoons, personnel records, and articles about UNIX torn out of magazines.

Most people avoid that kind of mess…er, filing system; instead, they develop an organizational scheme for all that paper.

Top 10 Ways To Deal with Office Paper

10. If it looks like it comes from headquarters, toss it out immediately.

9. Post it on the bulletin board, especially if it is potentially embarrassing to someone you hate.

8. Pile it in a stack on your desk. When the stack threatens to topple, toss the whole thing in the trash.

continues

Top 10 Ways To Deal with Office Paper (continued)

7. Add it to the stack on your coworker's desk.

6. Recycle it!

5. Make it into an airplane and launch it out the top floor window.

4. Store it in some semi-permanent way. For example, you could tape it to the bottom of a desk drawer.

3. Shred it.

2. Is it confidential? Photocopy it after hours, but leave it on the photocopier.

1. Fax it to the coast.

The most common way to deal with this abundance of papers, however, is to store it in file drawers, inside manila folders with labels on them. Sometimes, the manila folders are nested inside other folders—I like the hanging kind in multicolors!

Visually oriented people may file all blue paper in one folder and all shiny paper in another, but most of us tend to come up with better categories than that.

UNIX thinks of these "folders," into which information is organized, as *directories*. Don't confuse this with the kind of directory in which you can look up a friend's phone number or the name of the Kokomo, Indiana, chapter of the Lion's Club.

BUZZWORDS

DIRECTORY

A *directory* can be thought of as space on the computer into which related information is grouped so that you can find it when you need it.

Whether you think of directories as branches of a tree or folders in a file drawer, it's possible to divide directories further into subdirectories.

BUZZWORDS

SUBDIRECTORY

Directories contained within other directories are called subdirectories.

Inside each subdirectory, you can place additional subdirectories. You can do this *ad nauseam*, like a set of those Russian nesting dolls—directories within directories within directories.

Every UNIX disk has at least one directory, called the *root*, which is signified by a forward slash (/). The *root directory* in a UNIX system is the main disk (or directory) on which everyone's stuff is stored—everyone, that is, who has an account on the system to which the disk belongs. All information on the disk is located by its relationship to the root directory. Everything else on the disk, including the information you save there, is a branch coming off that root. The following figure shows a schematic of a UNIX file system, using the tree metaphor.

A UNIX file system tree. The root (/) is at the top.

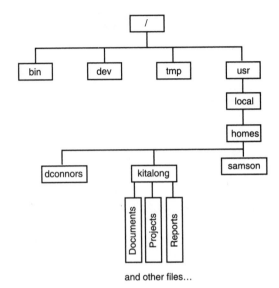

and other files...

If you have a graphical user interface (GUI), such as Open Windows or the X Window System, it can help you understand how the files are organized. Chapter 5 describes GUIs in some detail. Here's how the Open Windows GUI represents the hierarchical file system shown in the preceding figure:

An Open Windows GUI representation of the UNIX hierarchical file system.

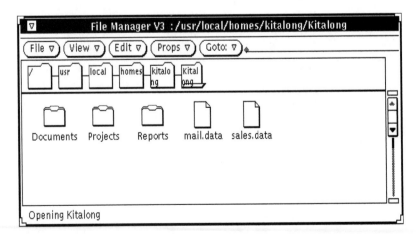

Is it becoming clearer? Let's try one more file system representation. This time, let's look at another level of the overall UNIX system. Take the diagram in the previous figure and expand the /usr directory.

The subdirectories and files within /usr contain software, user's files, local development projects, and so on.

TIP

> The directory name "/usr" tells us that the usr directory is one level below the root directory (/). If you want to sound like you know what you're talking about, pronounce this directory "slash user."

To describe the location of an individual's home directory as it relates to the /usr directory, you provide a *path name*, which describes the route one should take to get to the person's home directory. The *path* to a typical home directory within /usr might look something like this:

```
/usr/local/homes/kitalong
```

The directory labeled "kitalong" is one of a series of subdirectories within the /usr directory. If you want to be technically correct, you would say that all directories below the root are directories in their own right and subdirectories with respect to root.

BUZZWORDS

ABSOLUTE PATH

> The path name /usr/local/homes/kitalong is called an *absolute path*, because it describes precise directions for getting from the root directory to the directory of the person whose login id is kitalong. The first / in a path name always signifies the root directory, but the other /s are just punctuation marks that separate the directory levels.

The directory that bears your id is called your *home directory*. When you work on your UNIX system, the files and directories you create are stored in your home directory.

Below the directory level are regular files. In the paper-file example used earlier, files are those pieces of blue, white, and shiny paper that accumulate in your office. Each piece of paper, or file, is a collection of information that has to be put somewhere.

Files accumulate on computer disks, just as they do on your desk. Like paper files, computer files need to be put where they can be found again.

Most of the time, papers that aren't thrown away, shredded, or recycled find their way into a folder. Likewise, on computer systems, files often find themselves stored inside a directory or subdirectory.

OK. That's as clear as mud. Of what possible use is the information you've just read? The next section provides a clue.

Telling UNIX Where You Want To Go

In your file cabinet at the office, you have reason to rifle through files, for example, looking for a piece of green paper you've accidentally filed with the blue paper. Likewise, in UNIXland, you sometimes have reason to look inside directories, display the contents of a directory, move a file from one directory to another, relabel a directory or file, and so on.

Moving between Directories

In the real world, a CD is something you listen to and try to keep from spilling Coke on. Or it's a way of storing some extra money, to give you sweet—if fruitless—dreams of future riches. In UNIXland, cd is not that

exciting. It's just the command for changing directories. Try it. Remember the /usr directory that was the star of the preceding example? Why not go to that directory? Here's the command:

```
cd /usr
```

Oh, nooooo! How to get back home again? UNIX is satisfied with a plain

```
cd
```

or

```
cd ~
```

TIP

> Whenever you're lost in UNIXland, type **cd** or **cd** ~ and you are back in your home directory again. That squiggle is a tilde, pronounced "til-duh."

Another useful command is cd .., which moves you up one level in the UNIX file hierarchy. Try it now:

```
cd ..
```

Remember, to go back home again, just type cd or cd ~ and press Enter!

Listing the Contents of Directories

Did you get back home safely? Good. Now, to go back to the /usr directory and see what's inside it, type the following:

```
cd /usr
ls
```

Remember, `ls` is the command used to list files. Here's what some of the files in a typical /usr directory might look like.

```
5bin        dict      lib           old       sys
5include    etc       local         openwin   tmp
5lib        export    lost+found    pub       ucb
adm         games     man           sccs      ucblib
```

If you see something that looks intriguing, just `cd` to it. For example, the command to check out the /usr/bin directory is

```
cd bin
```

What happened to the /? Well, since you're already in the /usr directory, you don't have to give an absolute path name to move around within that directory. Without the /, UNIX assumes that you mean the sub-directory called "bin" within the current directory. If you type `cd /bin`, UNIX looks for the bin directory just below root—and probably doesn't find it.

If you like to type, UNIX understands if you type the whole path name, even if you're inside a directory that the path encompasses. So, for example, if you are inside the /usr directory and you want to be inside the bin subdirectory under /usr, UNIX puts you there if you type `cd /usr/bin`. But why do all that extra typing?

TIP

If you try to cd to something that's not a directory, UNIX gives you an error message, which looks something like this:

```
cd mail.data
mail.data: Not a directory
```

Identifying Where You Are
(Help! I'm lost!)

With all that cd-ing, remembering where you are can get complicated. So if you get lost in UNIXland, or want to know how far you have come in your travels before you go home, there's a UNIX command to help you: pwd (print working directory). This command was first encountered in Chapter 1—here it is again!

The pwd command doesn't literally print the information on your printer; instead, it displays the entire path name of the current directory on-screen. Here's what it looks like:

```
pwd
/usr/bin
```

EXPERTS ONLY

Here's your history lesson for today. Why does "print" mean "write to screen"? Well, back when UNIX was invented, there weren't any screens! The only kind of terminal that users and UNIXheads had was a keyboard and a built-in printer. It looked something like a typewriter. When a user typed a command to the computer, the output would print on the paper in the terminal. Talk about using up trees! But that's one of the reasons that UNIX plays a stony and silent role.

Creating Directories

Now that you've seen how to navigate around your UNIX system, you have to learn how to arrange your UNIX space in a convenient way. To do this, you create directories in a hierarchical system that seems sensible to you, and then place your files into those directories.

95

To get a file into a directory, you can create the file and save it to the appropriate directory, or you can move the file from its original place into the desired directory. This chapter takes care of the second approach, moving existing files from place to place. If you're just getting started, you probably don't have many files to worry about right now. Soon, though, you can begin creating lots of files with your software and with a couple of commands you learn in the next chapter.

To create (make) a directory, use the `mkdir` command (it's short for *make directory*). You have to give the directory a name as you create it. It looks like this:

    mkdir *directoryname*

For example, if you want to create a directory called Promotions that lives in your home directory, you first make sure that you are in the home directory (by typing `cd`, `cd ~`, or, just to verify, `pwd`).

Next, type:

mkdir Promotions

UNIX simply creates the directory in its usual, silent way. The next time you issue the `ls` command from within your home directory, you see the Promotions directory along with all of your other files.

Rules for naming files and directories

✔ UNIX differentiates between upper- and lowercase letters, so *Top* and *top* are two different words in UNIXland.

✔ You can use any letter as part of a file or directory name.

✔ Many punctuation marks can be used in UNIX file or directory names. Punctuation marks that you *should not* use include the following:

> * ? ^ $; \ & ! | % ~

All of these have some special meaning in UNIXland. Actually, such punctuation marks confuse the shell, not UNIX. But we're splitting hairs again!

✔ Sometimes, UNIX limits you to 14-character file names. To be on the safe side, you might want to set a 14-character limit on yourself.

✔ In DOSville, the period (.) is a character that separates the file name from its three-character extension. In UNIXland, periods and other punctuation marks are treated as normal characters.

TIP

When you issue the ls command, UNIX doesn't differentiate between files and directories. There are ways to get around this problem, as you see in Chapters 8 and 14, when the ls command is discussed more fully. But here's a quick and dirty solution: Take advantage of UNIX's case-sensitivity. When you name directories, begin the names with a capital letter. Name files in all lowercase letters.

Unless you are the system administrator and have access to the root directory (*root access*), you can create directories only in your own home directory or in public spaces on the file system. Likewise, others cannot create files or directories in your home directory unless you specifically give them permission (see Chapter 14 for more information about file permissions).

Organizing Directories

Just as you have control over how your office files are arranged, you also determine how to arrange your computer space. When you determine what that organization should be, you can use a bunch of commands to make it happen.

One of the best of these is mv. The mv command takes care of moving files and subdirectories from one directory to another. It's also the command you use to rename a file or directory. Here's how you rename something:

```
mv old new
```

Simple, huh? Of course, you replace the word *old* with the name of an existing file that you want to rename and the word *new* with the new name you want to give it.

CAUTION

> Don't rename or move any files beginning with a period (.). (Examples are .cshrc and .login). These are system files; if they are supposed to be in your home directory, but aren't, your account doesn't work.

Here's a for instance. Let's say you were working on a report for your boss, Glen. The report is named report.4.glen. Suddenly, Glen gets the axe. Your new boss, Charmaine, still has to get the report. You want to wipe out all evidence that you ever knew Glen. All you have to do is type:

```
mv report.4.glen report.4.char
```

A quick `ls` of your home directory might show the following files:

```
board.report       report.q1
documents          report.q4
mail.data          report.4.char
```

OK, here's the other major use for the `mv` command. Notice that several report files are in the home directory that was just listed. There's report.4.char, board.report, report.q1, and report.q4. (Yikes! I wonder what happened to q2 and q3?)

It seems reasonable to store all the reports together in one directory. First, make a directory, called Reports, to store the report files in. (Note the use of the initial capital letter to signify a directory.)

```
mkdir Reports
```

Now, move the report files into the Reports directory. You can start with report.4.char and work your way through one at time, like this:

```
mv report.4.char Reports

mv report.q1 Reports

mv report.q4 Reports

mv board.report Reports
```

You *could* do it that way. But that is a lot of typing. Unless you're working on your typing skills, you might want to try a shortcut that lets you move, in one fell swoop, all the files that contain the word *report*. Here's how it works:

```
mv *report* Reports
```

The asterisk (*) is a kind of wild card. (More about wild cards in Chapter 19.) With it, the command says to UNIX, "Move all the files with file names that contain the word *report* into the directory called Reports."

This may seem obvious, but I'm going to tell you anyway: You have to make a directory before you can move files into it.

TIP

In UNIXese, an asterisk (*) is called a *splat*. So, to impress your UNIX-speaking friends, you pronounce the previous command like this: "Move splat-report-splat Reports." If you really want to be impressive, say "cap-r-reports" instead of just plain "reports."

Check your work by listing the files in your directory:

```
ls
```

Here's what it might look like after the move:

```
Reports        documents        mail.data
```

CAUTION

A good way to lose files is to mistype the destination name. For instance, if you type mv `report.q4 reports`, UNIX thinks you wanted to give report.q4 the new name, "reports." That's because UNIX's case-sensitivity causes it to make a distinction between "reports" and "Reports."

Is that enough stuff about organizing your files by renaming them and moving them around? Let's go on to removing files.

Removing Files and Directories (You're outta here!)

When I'm working on a big project, I often save all the drafts of my work until I get final approval. Then, if I'm on the ball, before I completely forget the project and get on with something else, I clean out all the earlier drafts and just retain the final. So, on my disk right now, I have files named chapter7.dr1, chapter7.dr2, and chapter7.fin. Now that the book is published, all I really need is the chapter7.fin file, so I want to get rid of the two earlier drafts. The command is rm (short for remove). To remove chapter7.dr1, type:

```
rm chapter7.dr1
```

Ordinarily, UNIX simply zaps the file without further ado. But system administrators frequently set the rm command to "interactive" mode to prevent you from accidentally removing files that you want to keep.

If interactive remove is set up on your system, when you issue the rm command, you receive a message from UNIX asking if you're sure you want to remove the file. It looks something like this:

```
Remove chapter7.dr1? (y/n)
```

If you type y, the file is gone forever. If you type n, the rm command is ignored. This is especially useful if you take advantage of shortcuts, like the splat (*).

If interactive remove isn't set, what happens if I foolishly type:

```
rm chapter7*
```

The answer is all of my hard work on Chapter 7, including the final version, is gone forever. UNIX zaps the files in silence and without warning. The next time I look for chapter7.fin, it is gone, gone, gone.

If interactive remove is set, however, UNIX gives me a chance to notice that I had demanded the removal of all Chapter 7 files.

How to check for interactive *rm*

✔ Try the rm command on your system by removing a file that you don't care about.

✔ If you care about all your files, create an empty file called "test" by typing:

```
touch test
```

Then type:

```
rm test
```

Did you get a confirmation prompt? Then you're in business.

✔ If you didn't get a confirmation prompt, you can force UNIX to double-check with you before removing files. Use the interactive (i) option, instead of the plain vanilla rm command:

```
rm -i test
```

EXPERTS ONLY

> If your system administrator resists implementing rm -i across the whole system, you can make rm -i your own default by creating an alias for your account. See Chapter 18 for more information about aliases.

Just in case you haven't figured it out, IT IS NEVER A GOOD IDEA TO TYPE:

    rm *

DO NOT TRY THIS AT HOME, OR ANYWHERE ELSE!!

CHAPTER 8
Fiddling with Files

IN A NUTSHELL

▼ Listing files
▼ Creating files
▼ Copying files
▼ Linking files
▼ Finding lost files

F iddling with files means looking at them, creating them, duplicating them, losing them, finding them—as well as moving and removing them, as you learned in Chapter 7. You always have reason to fiddle with your files; in fact, the more familiar you become with UNIXland, the more dissatisfied you will be with the way you initially set up your file hierarchy.

This chapter also explains how to find lost files. Someday you will need this capability. Eventually, even *you* will file something and be unable to locate it again, either because you gave it a stupid name that doesn't reflect its contents, or because you put it in a directory with a stupid name, or because you flat out filed it in the wrong place. For those moments when you're most human—you learn the UNIX `find` and `grep` commands.

Listing Files

Listing files is the first step to fiddling with them. If you don't know what files you have, how can you fiddle? (Unless you're into fiddling in the dark, which can be dangerous.) To review the fascinating `ls` command, type the following:

    ls

Yep. It still lists the files in your current directory, as in this example:

    Documents   mail.data   report.4.char   sales.data

Remember those command options you learned about in Chapter 7? Let's look at one again, to get a handle on exactly what the output of some of those options mean to you. How about the `long` (`l`) option of the `ls` command:

    ls -l

That long list of files in your home directory gives you a lot of information:

```
total 4
drwxr-xr-x  2 kitalong  512  Nov 10  14:22  Documents
-rw-r--r--  1 kitalong  272  Nov 18   8:05  mail.data
-rw-r--r--  1 kitalong  536  Dec  5  19:02  report.4.char
-rw-r--r--  1 kitalong  138  Dec 14  14:53  sales.data
```

Interpreting the information in the *ls -l* command output

✔ `total 4` at the top of the file list could be construed as the number of files in the directory. In this case, `total 4` does correspond to the 4 files. However, this isn't a file head count. Instead, it's the amount of disk space occupied by the directory. Disk space is measured in blocks that are 4,096 bytes large.

✔ *First column:* Displays the permissions, which you learn more about in Chapters 13 and 14. For now, it's enough if you notice that the directory, named Documents, is distinguished by the letter d in the first column, whereas the other files simply have a - in that column.

✔ *Second column:* Counts the number of links to the file (UNIX is big on counting stuff—typical computer thing). You learn more about links later in this chapter. Notice that the directory is the only file that has more than one link right now.

✔ *Third column:* The owner's login id.

✔ *Fourth column.* Displays the file's size. None of these files is very large. A directory's size starts at 96 bytes and grows as you add files to it.

✔ *Fifth and sixth columns:* Displays the date and time the file was last modified.

continues

✔ *Seventh column:* The name of the file or directory itself. Yep, they're in alphabetical order, but the directory, because its name is capitalized, appears at the beginning of the list, thanks to UNIX's case-sensitivity.

If you want to see absolutely ALL the files in your home directory, the `ls` command's `a` and `A` options are for you. (Some versions of UNIX may not support the `ls -A` command—so if it doesn't work, it's not your fault!)

These options modify the `ls` command to show the regular files, plus any system files—those files that begin with a period—in your home directory. The `a` option also shows the **.** and **..** files, which signify the current and parent directory, respectively.

```
ls -a

.              .login        report.4.char
..             Documents     sales.data
.cshrc         mail.data
```

If you want to see the system files, but not the **.** and **..** directories, use the `-A` option for the `ls` command.

In some versions of UNIX, the `ls` command with the `-l` option works with the `-g` option to tell you the group affiliation of the person who owns the file. Again, this information is especially useful in conjunction with knowledge about permissions and file ownership, which are covered in Chapters 13 and 14. Here's the output of the `ls -lg` command:

```
total 4
drwxr-xr-x  2 kitalong  staff  512  Nov  10  14:22  Documents
-rw-r—r—    1 kitalong  staff  272  Nov  18   8:05  mail.data
-rw-r—r—    1 kitalong  staff  536  Dec   5  19:02  report.4.char
-rw-r—r—    1 kitalong  staff  138  Dec  14  14:53  sales.data
```

The -t option of the ls command sorts your files by time, displaying the most recently modified file or directory first. This is useful if you have a lot of files and you're trying to find a particular one that you know you worked on in the past couple of days. As soon as you see the file name, you remember it, right?

The recursive option (-R) of the ls command is also pretty neat. It lists the files in the current directory, and then goes on to list the contents of any subdirectories it finds. Here's what the output of the ls -R command looks like:

```
Documents    Projects    Reports    mail.data    sales.data

Documents:

text1

Projects:

xxx        yyy

Reports:

board.report    report.4.char    report.q1        report.q4
```

Creating Files

You can create files in UNIXland in a variety of ways.

✔ *With an editor like vi.* Chapters 10 through 12 introduce you to vi; don't try to deal with it right now, unless you've had prior experience using it.

✔ *With a normal software package.* "Normal" software is anything you use in your day-to-day activities: word processing programs, spreadsheets, painting or drawing programs, electronic mail programs, mathematical or statistical programs, you name it. If you use it for your work, somewhere files are being created and updated!

✔ *With the `touch` command.* The `touch` command creates an empty file, which you can use for practice. It has other uses, too; shell programmers, for example, use `touch` to update the date on a file without changing its contents. So if you want to create some empty files to fiddle with, go to the UNIX prompt and type something like `touch junk1`. When you list your files, it should be there. You notice a `0` in the size column if you do the `-l` option of the `ls` command.

✔ *With the `cat` command.* The `cat` command is another way to create files that you can fiddle with. It can also be used to create real, honest-to-goodness files that are of some usefulness later on. The `cat` command is described in the next section.

Using *cat* To Create and Update Files

The `cat` (short for *catenate* or *concatenate*) command is used as a quick and dirty way of creating short files. Here's how to use the `cat` command to create a file:

```
cat > useless.file
```

The UNIX prompt disappears, and you are cat-ing. Type anything. It appears on-screen. Press Enter whenever you want to start a new line. After you finish entering stuff into the file, press Enter and then press Ctrl-d (hold down the Ctrl key, then type the letter *d*). Ctrl-d is an end-of-file mark that tells UNIX you want to close and store the current file. UNIX responds to Ctrl-d by creating useless.file in the current directory.

CAUTION

If you already have a file called useless.file in your current directory, the cat command empties that file and fills it with the new text. Be careful when you're cat-ting around!!

If you want to look at the file you just cat-ted, type:

```
cat useless.file
```

Quiz: How observant are you? Did you notice what's different between the cat command that creates a file and the cat command to view a file?

Answer: Of course you caught it—it's the redirection symbol (>), which you used while creating the file but omitted while viewing.

If you went crazy and created an extremely long file—so long, in fact, that the whole thing could not appear on-screen at once—you could "pipe it to more." Yeah, right. Jargon check!

BUZZWORDS

PIPE

Technically, a *pipe* lets you use the output of one command as the input for a different command. So "pipe it to more" means to issue a command, like cat, and send the output of that command to another command for processing.

I HATE UNIX!

Here's how the `cat` command piped to `more` works. You know what the `cat` command does. What does `more` do? It displays something until the screen is full, and then waits to give you time to read the screen. When you're ready, you press the space bar. Then, `more` displays the next screen of information. Neat, huh?

TIP

The `more` command is built right into `man`, as you may recall from experimenting with `man` in previous chapters.

So if you want to pipe the `cat` command to the `more` command, type:

```
cat useless.file ¦ more
```

That straight vertical bar is the *pipe symbol*—appropriate, since it looks kinda like a drainpipe or something.

If you want to add some more stuff to useless.file, the `cat` command takes on a slightly different form:

```
cat >> useless file
```

Now, when you type more stuff into the file, it gets appended to the end of the file. Just press Enter and then Ctrl-d again to save it.

Three variations of the *cat* command

✔ To create a file: `cat > ` *newfile*

✔ To view a file: `cat ` *newfile*

✔ To add to a file: `cat >> ` *newfile*

Now, use `touch` or `cat` to create some files that you can play with. Or, use `touch` to create an empty file, and then add to it by using `cat` with two redirection symbols after it, like this:

```
touch stupid.file
cat >> stupid.file
```

Copying Files

Copying files is easy. A few rules prevail:

The four commandments of file copying

✔ Thou shalt not copy a file onto itself. (UNIX protests if you try to do so.)

✔ Thou shalt not copy a file and give it the same name as a directory. (Remember, in UNIX's powerful one-track mind, files and directories are the same thing.)

✔ Thou shalt not copy files that belong to others without their permission. (Even though you can use the `cd` command to change to other people's directories and the `ls` command to list their files, you have no business doing so unless they say it's OK.)

✔ Thou shalt not fill all available disk space with copies of files!

Copying Files in Your Home Directory

In its simplest form, the copy command looks like this:

```
cp file1 file2
```

For example, if you want to make a copy of useless.file and keep the copy in the same directory as the original, the command is

```
cp useless.file useless.again
```

You also can make a copy of useless.file, in another directory, for example, Reports. If you do that, you don't have to change its name, because the directory name, Reports, becomes part of its name, distinguishing it from the original useless.file you created in your home directory. So, here's how to copy a file into a different directory:

```
cp useless.file Reports
```

You can see that copies of useless.file easily could proliferate and take over your disk. Be sure to review the rm command in Chapter 7, so you can clean up the mess you make with all this cat-ing, cp-ing, and touch-ing.

Copying Files from Someone Else's Directory to Yours

Okay, now you know how to copy files in your home directory. But what if you want to copy a file that isn't in your home directory? It might be the case that you and Ted Samson (whose login id is samson) are working on a project together, and both of you want to work on the files related to the project. If Ted's home directory is on the same network as yours, you can use the cd (change directory) command to get to his directory, then use the cp command to copy a file back to your home directory.

I HATE UNIX!

First, `cd` to Ted's directory, using the ~ that you learned about in Chapter 7.

As you know, `cd` ~ means "change to my home directory." When the ~ precedes the name of another user on the network, it means "the home directory of" that person. So here's how you change to Ted's directory:

```
cd ~samson
```

Now, you can `ls` the files in Ted's home directory if you want. Here's an example of the `ls` command:

```
big.project       poem.4.gina       status.report
```

CAUTION

You immediately recognize that big.project is the file you're looking for. Wouldn't it be fun to succumb to temptation, and sneak a peek at the poem.4.gina that Ted is obviously writing? NONONONONO. The Golden Rule applies here—"Do unto others as you would have them do unto you." Furthermore, it might be illegal and maybe you might find out something you don't want to know.

To copy big.project back to your home directory, type:

```
cp big.project ~
```

Now you have a copy of big.project, and so does Ted. Before the temptation overcomes you and you read his poem.4.gina, get the heck out of there by typing:

```
cd ~
```

Unfortunately, if Ted makes changes to the `big.project` file in his home directory, they are not reflected in your copy, and vice versa. File linking can fix that dilemma; if you're interested, read the next section about the `ln` command.

TIP

Unless Ted sets his file permissions to give you write access to his home directory (not a good idea), you can't copy your files into his home directory. He has to do the copying into his directory. See Chapters 13 and 14 for more on file permissions.

File Linking with *ln*

When several people are working on a project together, it is useful for a copy of project documents to be accessible from each person's home directory. The copy command works OK, but it doesn't allow updates to be reflected automatically in each copy of the file. Linking, however, allows automatic updates by establishing a *pointer* that looks and acts like a copy of the master file. Each person who has a pointer in his or her home directory can read and write to the master file as though they owned it. However, only one copy of the master file exists.

You easily can establish a link to a file in your own home directory. Say that you wanted to put a copy of a file named 1994budget, which is customarily in your Budgets directory, into a project directory called Grants, so that you easily can access the budget while working on a grant proposal. The procedure is explained in the following sections.

Linking Files in Your Own Home Directory

The file to which you want to establish a link is Budgets/1994budget, and you want to create a link pointer called Grants/1994budget. The command looks like this:

```
ln -s Budgets/1994budget Grants/1994budget
```

So the syntax is

```
ln -s origfile newfile
```

The `-s` option makes it a *symbolic link*.

Hard links are also possible; if you want to use them, get some help from your resident UNIX expert.

BUZZWORDS

SYMBOLIC LINK

A *symbolic link* is a fake file or directory that points to another real file or directory somewhere else. A symbolic link is like a regular file, in that it has a name and location in the file system. But unlike a regular file or directory, a symbolic link has no contents of its own. It simply serves as a pointer to another file or directory.

Now, if you issue the command `ls -F Grants`, you see the following:

```
Appendices/    1994budget@    nsfgrant.draft1
```

The `-F` option of the `ls` command marks different types of files; as you can see, the directory Appendices is marked by a trailing slash, and the link is marked by a trailing @ sign.

Establishing Links between Home Directories

You can also establish a link to a file in another person's directory on your file system.

I HATE UNIX!

CHAPTER 8

Start by making sure you have write and execute permission on the file to which you want to establish the link. File permissions are explained in Chapters 13 and 14 of this book. The only person who can change permissions is the file's owner, so have him or her read Chapters 13 and 14 of this book, if necessary.

Now link the file named big.project in Ted Samson's home directory to my home directory. The command looks like this:

```
ln -s ~samson/big.project ~/samson.proj
```

Issuing the `ls -F` command in my home directory verifies that samson.proj is, indeed, a symbolic link. It looks and acts like an actual file, but is only a pointer to the real file in Ted's directory.

Breaking the Link

When the project is complete, I can delete the symbolic link by typing:

```
rm samson.proj
```

If Ted deletes or moves the master file, UNIX is confused, because symbolic links aren't deleted automatically with their master files. Ted and I must both understand this quirk of the `ln` command, so we don't inadvertently confuse UNIX by deleting or moving our linked files.

Finding Lost Sheep

As you might imagine, misplacing files in UNIXland is not too hard. All you have to do is make a teeny little typing error. Because the UNIX inventors occasionally lost files themselves, they created two commands, `grep` and `find`, for locating wayward information.

Finding Files with the *find* Command

If you can remember the name of the file you lost, the `find` command helps you. Like many UNIX commands, `find` has many options. You don't need to know all of them, but a couple of strategies are helpful.

If you want UNIX to start from the current working directory and search for a file named project.list, type:

```
find . -name project.list -print
```

Yeah, yeah. What does it all mean? Well, `find` is fairly obvious. The `.` tells UNIX to begin its search "right here," in the current working directory. Next, `-name` is an option that tells UNIX that the next thing in the command is the name of a file. Next, of course, is the file name, followed by another option, `-print`, which tells UNIX to print the path name of the file (on-screen, not on a printer).

You can narrow or broaden the search by replacing the `.` with other things. For example, to search the entire file system beginning with the root directory, type:

```
find / -name project.list -print
```

Similarly, to search within a particular directory, type the full path name of the directory:

```
find /usr/local/homes/kitalong -name project.list
-print
```

If you know only part of the file name, you can use the * as a wild card. For example, if you know that the word "project" is in the file name but you don't know what the rest of the name is, try this:

```
find /usr/local/homes/kitalong -name "*project*" -print
```

If you're searching a wide area, like the entire disk, or if you're searching using wild cards, the likelihood increases that your search will turn up many files. If you think you will find a lot of files, append ¦ more to the end of the command, to display only a screen of information and then pause. When you're ready to move on, you can press the space bar. Here's what the find command looks like, starting from the root directory (/), and tacking ¦ more onto the end:

```
find / -name project.list -print ¦ more
```

Finding Directories with the *find* Command

The find command is also used to find lost directories, but with a minor change or two. Here's how to find a directory called Projects and print the location on-screen, starting from the root:

```
find / -name Projects -type d -print
```

How *find* Works

What happens when you issue a find command? UNIX looks for files with that name in the area in which you directed it to search. When it finds such a file, it prints the name to the screen and keeps looking. It doesn't stop until it has gone through all the subdirectories and files in the search path. This could take a long time. If you get bored or give up all hope of ever finding the lost file, or if—wonder of wonders—the file you are seeking is actually found, you usually can stop the find command by pressing Ctrl-c. In other words, hold down the key marked Control or Ctrl, and then press the letter c on the keyboard. If Ctrl-c doesnt work, try the Delete key (sometimes labeled Del).

The find command has many other useful options. You can learn about them by typing:

```
man find
```

Getting a *grep*
(Finding lost files when the name escapes you, but the content doesn't)

A month or so ago, you were working on a proposal for a new personnel system. The proposal is due next week, but you can't find your draft—probably because, while studying UNIX, you learned the `mv` and `mkdir` commands and rearranged all your work. What to do, what to do? Well, can you remember any distinctive word or phrase from the document? How about the phrase *personnel system*?

If you have any recollection about the lost file's content, the `grep` command can help you find it. Here's an example of the `grep` command:

```
grep "personnel system" *
```

The command tells `grep` to look for the phrase *personnel system* in all the files in the current working directory.

BUZZWORDS

SEARCH STRING

The term "`personnel system`" in this example is known as the search string. The quotation marks are necessary because a space is in the search string. If you're looking for a single word, quotation marks aren't necessary.

When grep has located the words *personnel system*, it prints the name of any files containing the string along with the relevant line or lines of the file. It looks something like this:

```
people.R.Us: The new personnel system will accomplish
char.memo: chance to work on the new personnel system
```

As a UNIX command, grep is accustomed to distinguishing between upper- and lowercase letters. The i (ignore) option tells grep to ignore this distinction. The command

```
grep -i doorknobs *
```

might produce the following response:

```
people.R.Us: Doorknobs will no longer receive raises.
house.plans: 12 doorknobs @ $7.95
```

Don't be distressed by this lengthy description of how to find lost files. Everyone who uses UNIX has lost a file at some time; otherwise, you wouldn't be blessed with such elaborate mechanisms for finding them again.

So you see, grep is not a rude noise made by a UNIX computer that has just swallowed all your files. In fact, it is an acronym for "globally search for a regular expression and print." In this case, the regular expression they're talking about is the search string.

CHAPTER 9

The Mysteries of Printing

IN A NUTSHELL

▼ Where do printouts go?
▼ Stopping runaway print jobs
▼ Batch printing

W hen everyone has a computer on his or her desk and a printer on a table next to the desk, printing works pretty smoothly. The only stumbling blocks might be getting the two pieces of hardware to speak intelligibly to each other in the first place and getting new software to work with the printer. At best, a few rough moments are likely. At worst, printing never works at all, but this is rare.

When your computer and printer are both parts of a network, however, it's a little more complex. This chapter gives you some insight into how printing works under UNIX System V Release 4(SVR4), especially when your computer is part of a network. The objective is to keep you from having to walk distractedly from printer to printer looking for your printouts.

EXPERTS ONLY

Printing is one of the areas of profound difference between Berkeley UNIX and SVR4 UNIX. Although the end user may not notice anything at all, the system administrator converting to SVR4 has a lot of learning to do.

Where Do Printouts Go?

Printouts are sent to local or remote printers.

BUZZWORDS

LOCAL and REMOTE PRINTERS

A *local printer* is attached directly to your computer or to your local-area network and is directly accessible by you. If you want to use a local printer while connected to the network, the network has to know about that printer. This means that the system administrator must go through a rather complicated process of "registering" the printer and configuring it for network access.

I HATE UNIX!

A *remote printer* is attached to a local-area network that isn't a part of your immediate surroundings. The printer is accessible from your computer, though, because the two LANs can communicate with each other. Again, the system administrator must go through a process of "registering" the other LAN and the printer, so that your LAN knows about it.

Remote printing often is used when your company only has one photo-typesetter or color plotter. For special jobs, you can use your remote printing capabilities just for final drafts, while you send rough copy to your local printer for proofing.

If you have direct access to UNIX (through your PC or workstation), more often than not you use your word processing, e-mail, spreadsheet, graphic design, or other software package to manage the printing of your files. All UNIX-based software packages come equipped with built-in menu access to the UNIX print command.

If you have to dial in from a terminal, however, you will be glad for the versatile UNIX print command (`lp`), which lets you print text files you create with `cat` (see Chapter 8) or with `vi` (see Chapters 10 through 12). With some of the options of the print command, you also can print special kinds of files if you have the proper type of printer.

Most networked printers are equipped with a capability called *print spooling*.

HUH?

BUZZWORDS

SPOOLING and PRINT QUEUES

When many people send files to one printer, a print spooler is needed to keep order—to line up the files waiting to be printed and send them to the printer one by one. Spooling is a

continues

continued

way of storing files until they're ready to be processed. Print spooling is a particular type of spooling. Sometimes print spooling is handled by the printer itself, but more often, the print spooling software lives on the UNIX server that runs your network.

The lineup of jobs waiting to be printed is called the *print queue* (*queue* is pronounced just like the letter "Q").

In UNIX System V Release 4 (SVR4), the print command is

```
lp filename
```

So, to print a file named useless.file, type:

```
lp useless.file
```

UNIX returns a message like the following:

```
Request id is laser01-18 (1 file)
```

This request id number is important to you later if you want to stop a print job after you've sent it to the printer. You don't have to memorize it, but be aware that it exists.

In case you need a mnemonic device to help you remember the print command, the letters lp stand for *line printer*. Nowadays, hardly anyone uses line printers except for very mundane work. In our office, for example, a line printer tracks system input and output; the system administrator pays attention to those printouts only if something goes wrong. Therefore, since laser printers have become the standard in most offices, you can pretend that the lp command stands for *laser printer*, if you like!

TIP

If `lp` doesn't work for you, maybe you're not using SVR4. Try the `lpr` command, which is common in Berkeley UNIX.

But we still haven't answered the question, "Where do printouts go?" That's because there isn't a simple answer. If you have a small UNIX network with only one printer on it, it's easy to find out. Even if the printer is in a room down the hall, if it's the only printer on your network, it's bound to be the one that earns the right to print your file.

If you have more than one printer on your network, your inner Sherlock Holmes needs to kick in.

"I HATE THIS!"

Where the heck is my printout??!!!

✔ *Trial-and-Error Method I:* Try the printer nearest your office.

✔ *Trial-and-Error Method II:* Go from printer to printer, checking for your printout; it's got to be somewhere!

✔ *Scientific Deduction Method I:* Issue the lpstat -d command, which tells you the name of your default printer.

✔ *Scientific Deduction Method II:* Change your default printer to one you like better.

The Printer Nearest Your Office

Most likely, the system administrator who set up your system chose one printer as the default printer for everyone in the work area, or designated a nearby printer as your default printer. Unless the majority of your

printing is very specialized—involving forms, publication-quality photo-typesetting, or graphics plotting—this default printer is probably a dot-matrix, inkjet, or laser printer.

Other Available Printers

If your default printer isn't the one nearest your office, it might be that you are one of those lucky people whose work involves a great deal of special forms or documents that require special handling. In that case, a printer somewhere in your area probably handles such specialized printing. Find it.

If you don't have special printing needs, but your system administrator has designated a printer for you that is very far away from your office, perhaps your system administrator has a good reason. Find out what it is.

Printing as the cornerstone of the office wellness program

✔ The most likely reason for office printers to be far from the people they serve is that the system administrator is also the chairperson of the office wellness committee, and this is his way of ensuring that you get enough exercise. What to do?

✔ If you can't convince the sys-ad/wellness nut that he should set you up with a printer that's closer to your office, try to get him assigned to a different committee.

✔ If this doesn't work, sign up for noon-time aerobics to placate him.

✔ As a last resort, learn the -d (destination) option of the lp command and use it to send your printouts to a closer printer.

The *lpstat* Command

As you might infer from its name, `lpstat` supplies you with the status of your print jobs. The `lpstat` command gains added power when you use it with some of its options.

By itself, the `lpstat` command provides information about the jobs you have sent to the printer. The output of `lpstat` looks something like this, when your print job is still in the queue:

```
laser01     kitalong     138        Dec 2  15:33
```

If your job is actually printing, the `lpstat` output tells you so, as in this example:

```
laser01     kitalong     138        Dec 2  15:33      on laser01
```

Interpreting the output of the *lpstat* command

✔ *First column:* Tells you which printer is your default.

✔ *Second column:* Gives your login id.

✔ *Third column:* Gives you the size of the file in bytes (138 is very small—just a line or two of text).

✔ *Fourth column:* Gives the date and time when the file was sent to the printer.

✔ *Fifth column:* In the second example, the fifth column, on `laser01`, tells you that the file is now printing. The first example shows no fifth column, so you know that the file is still in the queue.

If your file has already been printed, `lpstat` is, in typical UNIX fashion, silent.

To find the location of your printouts, use `lpstat -d`, which tells you the name of your default destination printer. If you type

```
lpstat -d
```

UNIX responds with this:

```
system default destination: laser01
```

Changing Your Print Destination

To change your printer destination for a particular print job, use the following command syntax:

```
lp -d printername filename
```

Suppose that your normal (default) printer, which is a three-minute walk to the other side of the building, is named laser01. The printer to which you want to send your files is located closer, and is named laser02. The file you are trying to print is named useless.file.

As you may recall, the command to print useless.file to your default (aerobic) printer is

```
lp useless.file
```

If you want to send it to the laser02 (anaerobic) printer, the command look likes this:

```
lp -d laser02 useless.file
```

The `lp` command has many more options, which you can explore at your leisure. Type **man lp** for the full scoop.

```
LPDEST=laser02; export LPDEST
```

This makes laser02 your default printer, but only until you log out. To change it permanently, see the customization strategies in Chapter 18.

Stopping Runaway Print Jobs

To cancel a print job, you have to know the job's *request id*. As mentioned previously in this chapter, after you issue the command

```
lp useless.file
```

UNIX sends you the following message:

```
Request id is laser01-18 (1 file)
```

Notice that the request id includes the name of the printer, followed by a hyphen, and then a number that represents your printouts sequence in the lineup of print jobs that have been sent to the printer. In the example above, your file's request id is `laser01-18`.

The request id is the secret code you need to cancel a print job, whether the job has started printing or is still in the print queue. The cancel command looks like this:

```
cancel laser01-18
```

✔ If you mistakenly send a very long print job, you can stop it before it starts printing, or stop it in mid-print, before it uses up all the paper.

✔ After you've sent an important print job to a particular printer, if you realize that someone else is printing a long, graphically complex file, you can cancel your print job and send it to a different printer, rather than wait all day.

✔ You can cancel all your print jobs on a particular printer with the `cancel` *printername* command (such as `cancel laser01`).

Batch Printing

If your system administrator permits it, you can schedule print jobs for a later time by using a command intended for scheduling various types of jobs in UNIXland. The `at` command lets you state a command and a time at which it is to be issued.

For example, to print useless.file at 12:10 (when most everyone's out to lunch), use the following command:

```
at 1210pm < lp useless.file
```

To print the file on a day when everyone's out of the office, use a command like this:

```
at 10 Dec 11 < lp useless.file
```

The file will be printed at 10 a.m. on December 11.

Here are some important things to know about the at command:

✔ The at command has several options (surprise!).

✔ The at command accepts date and time information in many different formats, including

```
at now + 10 minutes

at 10 Dec 11 + 1 month

at 16

at 4pm
```

✔ The printer to which you want to send the printout must be turned on and on-line (UNIX does not turn it on or off for you). Make special arrangements with your system administrator before trying to execute the at command during off hours.

✔ You don't have to be logged in when the at command is executing.

Golden rules of UNIX printing

✔ When you're testing your printing, use a very small file, so as not to tie up the printer needlessly.

✔ If you have very large files to print, or files with lots of graphics in them, avoid the busiest time of the day. Come in early or stay late, use the at command, or warn your colleagues so that they can send their files to a different printer while your file is printing.

✔ The plain vanilla lp command is designed to print text files, not files you create with your software. You can use lp with an option or two to print software-created files, but this depends on what kind of files your software creates (an option exists for PostScript files, but don't count on options for all types of files).

continues

Golden rules of UNIX printing (continued)

✔ If your file prints out looking like pure garbage, it's probably because you used the plain vanilla lp command to print a software-created file, or because the printer to which you sent the file is not equipped to handle the file format you fed it. Experiment a bit more, or ask your system administrator for help.

PART III

Using vi, UNIX's Virtually Impossible Editor

Includes:

CHAPTER 10

vi Basics—No Pain, No Gain

IN A NUTSHELL

- ▼ Word processing versus vi
- ▼ Creating a file with vi
- ▼ Storing a file with vi
- ▼ Retrieving a file with vi
- ▼ Learning other vi commands

You can use a word processing program for many tasks. But there are times when you need a text editor to be empowered in the UNIX environment.

✔ Empowerment in UNIXland means being able to add commands, aliases, and customization to your login and system setup files without having to ask a system administrator to help you.

✔ Empowerment means being able to take advantage of some of the remote capabilities of UNIX, such as the ability to log in and read your mail while you're on the road.

✔ Empowerment means you don't have to do everything yourself: with an on-line calendar file, for example, anyone you authorize to do so—including your secretary and other staff members—can update your appointments and reminders.

✔ Empowerment means saving time by circulating first drafts in text format by way of e-mail, instead of working from possibly incompatible word processing programs.

✔ Empowerment means you can worry about the content, and let someone else worry about the format. Sometimes the software you use is not the best software for the job. But vi is good for first drafts of almost anything.

You may decide that you're not ready yet for the wonderful world of **vi**sual editing (also known as **vi**rtually **i**mpossible editing, **vi**cious editing, and other unprintable names). But if you are, this chapter is for you.

The first thing you need to learn about vi is how to pronounce it. A lot of people pronounce it to rhyme with "vie." This is acceptable, but brands you as someone who is not a true UNIX-geek. A few very odd people pronounce it "six" because of its visual affinity with the Roman numeral of the same name. But true-blue-UNIX-lovers say "vee-eye." Now you know.

Creating and Editing a File with vi

If you're using UNIX from a PC or terminal, you can work at any UNIX prompt. If you're using a Graphical User Interface, open a shell window to find a UNIX system prompt.

vi

This command opens a new file. The file is not named; you have to give it a name when you save it.

vi newfile

Use this version to simultaneously open a new file and give it a name. You'll have to be creative—don't use "newfile" for all your file names, although it'll work out OK the first time!

The figure shows an example.

A **vi** screen as it
appears when you open
it with **vi newfile**
(a named new file).

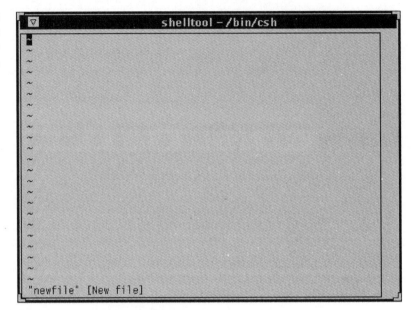

vi oldfile

Try this command to open an existing file in your home directory. The
cursor is at the beginning of the file.

If the file you want to open is not in the current directory, give the full
pathname. vi creates a new file if it can't find the one you want to open.

vi +$ oldfile

This version of vi oldfile opens an existing file and positions the cursor at the end of the file so you can immediately start working.

Changing Modes

When you start vi, you are automatically in command mode. Sometimes command mode is called edit mode; in fact, you may catch me using these two mode names interchangeably in this book. Don't hold it against me!

To add text to a file, you enter input mode by typing a lowercase i.

"I HATE THIS!"

I give up! What's a mode?

Modes are typical computer things. When computer programs can operate in more than one specific way, each way is called a mode. In vi, you have to switch back and forth between input mode and command (edit) mode. It's awkward, to say the least.

Pressing Esc (Escape on some keyboards) switches from input mode back to command (edit) mode so you can make changes to your file or give UNIX orders from the command line.

From command mode, pressing Esc followed by a colon (:) brings you to the command line, where you can issue file-level commands, like search, change, write, and quit.

Editing Commands

Typing x deletes the character under the cursor. Typing dw deletes the word that the cursor is currently in, but only from the cursor position over to the right. If you want to delete the whole word, make sure your cursor is on the first letter of the word.

Typing dd deletes the whole line that the cursor is on. It makes no difference where the cursor is positioned on the line.

Moving around in *vi*

To review files in vi, you use these keys:

✔ Arrow keys move the cursor from place to place. The line on which the cursor is positioned is known as the *current line*.

✔ Ctrl-u or Ctrl-b is used to scroll up (backward) through the file, a screen at a time. This method is faster than the arrow keys.

✔ Ctrl-d or Ctrl-f is used to scroll down (forward) through the file, a screen at a time. This method is faster than the arrow keys.

Saving and Exiting Files

When you are finished working on a file or in vi, or if you are still editing but want to save the changes you have made to this point, use these commands:

✔ q   Used from the command line—that is, after you've pressed Esc and then typed a colon (:)—this command lets you quit working on a file if you have made no changes to it.

✔ quit!   Used from the command line—that is, after you've pressed Esc and then typed a colon (:)—this command lets you quit working on a file without saving any changes you might have made. Use it if you want to revert to the way the file was before you last saved it, or when you first loaded it.

✔ w   This is another command-line command that lets you write (save) a file that already has a name. After you write the file, you remain in vi so you can continue editing.

✔ w *filename*   A command-line command that lets you save and name a new file or save and rename an old file that you are editing. After you write the file, you remain in vi so you can continue editing.

✔ wq   A command-line command that lets you write (save) and quit working on a file at the same time. After you issue this command, you return to the UNIX prompt.

✔ r *filename*   A command-line command that lets you bring in the contents of a different file and merge those contents with the contents of the file you have on-screen. The file is brought in immediately following the current cursor location.

✔ set showmode   If you have trouble remembering which mode (input or edit/command) you are in, go to the command line by pressing Esc followed by a colon (:). Then issue the set showmode command. The current mode is displayed in the lower right corner of the screen until you stop using vi.

More Retrieving and Editing Commands

The vi editor has so many commands that you cannot learn them all at once. After you've mastered basic editing functions, there are a few advanced commands that you will probably use immediately. Here are a handful of advanced vi (edit) mode commands to get you to the next level of expertise. All of these commands are issued while you are in command mode. They are not issued from the command line. To get to command mode, so that you can issue these commands, press Esc.

✔ **a**   An alternative to i; instead of opening up a space at the cursor position, it opens up a space immediately following the cursor position. Puts you in input mode.

✔ **A**   Opens up a space at the end of the line on which the cursor is positioned. Puts you in input mode.

✔ **$**   Brings your cursor to the end of the current line (the line your cursor is on).

✔ **r**   Replaces the character under the cursor with the character you type immediately after typing the r. For example, to change the word "burn" to "barn," you should be in command (edit) mode, then position your cursor on the *u* in burn, type a lowercase *r*, and immediately type the letter *a* without moving your cursor again. Voila!

✔ **R**   Puts you into typeover mode. Whatever you type replaces the characters that were there previously. To get out of this mode, press Esc.

✔ **o**   Adds an empty line below the line on which the cursor is currently positioned. o puts you in input mode so you can add text within the new line.

✔ **O**   Adds an empty line above the line on which the cursor is currently positioned. Puts you in input mode so you can add text within the new line.

✔ **yw**   "Yanks" or copies the word that your cursor is currently positioned in. The word isn't deleted; it's just copied, so that you can put it somewhere else.

✔ **Y**   "Yanks" or copies the entire line *on which your* cursor is positioned. The line isn't deleted; it's copied, so that you can put it somewhere else.

✔ p   "Puts" (inserts) the text previously "yanked" right after the current cursor position.

✔ P   "Puts" (inserts) the text previously "yanked" right before the current cursor position.

How To Learn the Other 5,006 (or so) *vi* Commands

There are many vi commands. Maybe not 5,006, but it seems like it. To learn them, you should wait until you want to do something that seems like a reasonable thing to do. Maybe it's something you've done in one of the software packages you use, or something you've seen a friend do with vi.

When you're ready for something new, ask someone, check a vi reference manual, or try ferreting out the information from the man pages.

If you use vi a great deal for very complex tasks, you undoubtedly need more depth than the commands presented in Chapters 10 through 12 can provide. But average UNIX users—those who have GUIs and word processing programs—are pretty much done learning vi. Some advice, though: Read the next couple of chapters and try the techniques. You will be glad for the extra vi practice they afford you.

CHAPTER 11

A Handful of Useful Things You Can Do with vi

IN A NUTSHELL

- ▼ Create a calendar
- ▼ Create text (ASCII) files
- ▼ Capture and edit command output
- ▼ Make a list that you can sort
- ▼ Combine a number of files into one

U sing your imagination with vi, you can probably adapt some of the suggestions in this chapter for your own use.

Create a Calendar

If you have a GUI, it probably comes with a fancy calendar program that displays actual calendar pages on-screen, lets you view a week, month, or day at a glance, and looks real pretty.

But it's going to be pretty much useless on the day you want to call in sick, but can't remember if there's anything vitally important you must do that day. If your calendar file is a plain ASCII file that you prepare with vi, however, you can use your modem to call in from home to check your calendar before you get your hopes up. You even can update your calendar file from home, a feat that is next to impossible with a GUI calendar program, unless you have access to fairly sophisticated networking equipment and software.

To create and use a calendar file, type **vi calendar** while you're in your home directory. Then enter reminders, one per line, in a variety of formats. There is no need to put them in any particular order; the `calendar` command sorts them for you, as long as each reminder is on a separate line, and you remember to press Enter after each one.

Here is a sample calendar file:

```
Dentist 8:30 a.m. February 23
Feb. 23  2 pm conference call with LA office
2/23 1 p.m. Sales meeting—bring 4Q figures
Feb. 23 19:00 Parents night at Joey's school
```

Each day, type `calendar` to remind you of your daily appointments. The calendar program makes use of the `grep` command that you learned in Chapter 8 to search through the file for all entries with the current date. Then, the program displays those entries on-screen for your convenience. The entries are displayed as you typed them. So your calendar for February 23 (shown in the preceding example) wouldn't look pretty, but it would get the job done.

If you use the calendar program regularly, you'll probably develop your own format for entering appointments so that the screen display is useful and convenient for you.

When you get to Chapter 18, you learn a couple of strategies for convincing the `calendar` command to run automatically when you log in.

Create Text (ASCII) Files

Often you want to share files with others who do not use the same word processing or spreadsheet software that you do. In this case an ASCII file is the only way to go!

BUZZWORDS

ASCII

ASCII (rhymes with passkey) stands for **A**merican **S**tandard **C**ode for **I**nformation **I**nterchange. *ASCII is a standard code used on most microcomputers, terminals, and printers to represent characters as binary digits. Because virtually all computers understand ASCII code, it is the common language for computer users.*

Luckily, vi is a master at creating ASCII files. Your word processor, on the other hand, creates a binary file that can only be used by people who have the same word processor. ASCII files can easily be shared over the network and included in electronic mail. When you are in the early stages of a project, you might want to use vi to create drafts in ASCII format, reserving the final formatting with your word processor for the last stage of the project, when the content is just how you want it.

Capture and Edit Command Output

One good reason to capture and edit command output is to help you explain a system problem to a programmer, system administrator, or other UNIX expert. Such people have difficulty dealing with comments like, "I haven't changed anything, but when I issued this command, I got really weird output." The expert is likely to perceive such comments as the mindless whining of a near-imbecile, and will probably say, in *that* tone of voice, "Exactly what output did you get?"

If you use UNIX to capture the troublesome output in a file, use vi to edit a little explanation into the output file, then e-mail the file to the expert; that expert will be much more able (and more willing) to help you.

To capture command output—for example, the output of the ps (process) command—you simply redirect it into a file, like this:

```
ps > process.file
```

This command creates a file that contains a list of the processes being executed on your system at the time the command is issued. (See Chapter 18 for a little more information about processes in UNIXland.)

Now, the file can be edited with `vi`:

```
vi process.file
```

You can add a short salutation at the beginning, followed by a few lines of explanation of what you perceived as weird about the command output. Then you can include the whole file in an e-mail message that you send to the expert.

Make a List of Stuff To Be Sorted

You don't need a fancy GUI tool to maintain an on-line address book. All you need is `vi` and the UNIX `sort` command.

The `sort` command rearranges the lines of a file in order by the first letter of each line. When the first letters are the same, sort compares the second letters, the third letters, and so on, using exactly the same strategy you'd use if you were sorting a list of stuff into alphabetical order. So, if you want to create an on-line address book, you can begin by creating a file called address.data (for lack of a more creative name).

```
vi address.data
```

Now, enter your friends' names and addresses, one per line, into the file. Don't worry about putting them in any particular order; just type them as you think of them.

```
Dumpty, Humpty. 420 Main Street, Egg Falls, VT
Thumb, Tom. RR1, Box 142, Littleville, MO
Grinch, Mr. 100 Third Street, Whoville, USA
Columbus, Chris. 91 Santa Maria Blvd., Columbus, OH
Mouse, Minnie. 1 Cheddar  Way, Orlando, FL
```

When you're finished typing, save the file. (Remember how? It's Esc-:-w-q.)

Next, just type:

```
sort address.data
```

The `sort` command will put the addresses in alphabetical order, like this:

```
Columbus, Chris. 91 Santa Maria Blvd., Columbus, OH
Dumpty, Humpty. 420 Main Street, Egg Falls, VT
Grinch, Mr. 100 Third Street, Whoville, USA
Mouse, Minnie. 1 Cheddar Way, Orlando, FL
Thumb, Tom. RR1, Box 142, Littleville, MO
```

Well, you're not quite finished. The `sort` command sorts the lines of the file, all right, but it just displays them on-screen. That is of little help for your alphabetized address book. What you really want is to sort the file. You could do the following:

```
sort -o address.data address.data
```

Whenever you add information to the address.data file, just re-sort it using the sort -o command, and you are in business.

If you want to sort a file in which some lines start with capital letters and some with lowercase letters, you have two choices. The following list, called party.stuff, can be alphabetized with upper- and lowercase letters mixed together or separated.

```
envelopes
Baskin-Robbins Ice Cream
Kleenex
boxes
spider webs
Tomatoes
```

The sort command without any options separates upper- and lowercase letters, putting the lines with lowercase letters first, in alphabetical order, followed by the lines beginning with uppercase letters, also in alphabetical order.

```
sort party.stuff > shopping list
Baskin-Robbins Ice Cream
Kleenex
Tomatoes
boxes
envelopes
spider webs
```

If you want all the words sorted together regardless of whether they begin with an upper- or lowercase letter, use the -f option of the sort command. (In this case, f stands for "fold," as in folding together ingredients for a cake.)

```
sort -f party.stuff > shopping.list
Baskin-Robbins Ice Cream
boxes
envelopes
Kleenex
spider webs
Tomatoes
```

"I HATE THIS!"

Why didn't it sort the way I expected?

If you want to sort a numbered list, beware. Take the seemingly ordinary list of numbers that any third grader could sort:

```
10
2
1
120
20
```

continues

Why didn't it sort the way I expected? (continued)

UNIX, if told to sort that list without any qualifying options, produces the following:

```
sort number.list
1
10
120
2
20
```

It's clear that UNIX doesn't understand. When faced with a sorting problem, it wants to treat numbers and letters the same, when everyone knows numbers demand a different approach. So, to get UNIX to put the numbers in the order you really want, you have to use the **sort -n** command. Typing:

```
sort -n number.list
```

produces:

```
1
2
10
20
120
```

Ahhh. That's better.

I HATE UNIX!

Combine a Number of Files into One

Of course, UNIX, in its infinite wisdom, offers many choices of how to merge data from several files into one file. Three choices, each useful in its own way, get you started. They are merging with the `sort` command, merging with the `cat` command, and merging with `vi`.

Merging and Sorting

Well, if you have several files that you want to merge into one, and you want to sort them in the process, the `sort` command has a merge option (`-m`). Let's say Joe and Jamie are getting married, and they want to combine their address books into one.

Newlyweds' guide to merging and sorting a combined address book

✔ First, they would probably copy the files into one home directory, to facilitate the merge and sort process.

✔ Next, they would weed out all the addresses of old boyfriends and girlfriends. The `dd` command in `vi` works for this.

✔ To verify that all of the old flames have been edited out, they each might want to sort their own address files individually first. The ordinary `sort` command works here.

When they finally have their two cleaned-up files—perhaps joe.addresses and jamie.addresses—they are ready to merge.

TIP

Betcha a dollar that one or the other—maybe even both—
saves the old flames' addresses in a separate file! Here's how
to do it: Copy the addresses file, move it to a hidden location
deep inside an unrelated subdirectory, and give it an innocu-
ous and uninviting name such as "1984inventory."

OK, now that Joe and Jamie have edited their address books and hidden
away the original copies for a rainy day, they are ready to put the files
together:

```
sort -m joe.addresses jamie.addresses > our.addresses
```

Or, maybe, to avoid domestic discord, they should alphabetize the file
names in the sort command, like this (although UNIX doesn't care
which comes first):

```
sort -m jamie.addresses joe.addresses > our.addresses
```

Merging with the *cat* Command

To merge several files with the cat command, just use the file names as
arguments for the command. The files appear on-screen in the order
indicated, if you type the following:

```
cat jamie.addresses joe.addresses
```

If you want to put the files together and store the combined files as a
new file, type:

```
cat jamie.addresses joe.addresses > our.addresses
```

After the files are concatenated with cat, the sort command can jump
in to sort them into alphabetical order.

If you're really adventurous, try cat-ting and sort-ing in one command, using a vertical bar (¦) called a *pipe*. The command looks like this:

```
cat jamie.addresses joe.addresses¦ sort-o our.addresses
```

Merging with vi

Getting vi to put two files together is a piece of cake. If you're vi-ing to merge, load one of the files into vi by typing:

vi *first.file*

(Of course, you would replace the words *first.file* with the name of the actual file.) Put your cursor at the point in the file at which you want to insert the contents of another file.

To get to the command line, press the Esc key followed by a colon. Then type:

r *second.file*

Again, you use the actual name of the second file here. The second file reads into the first file at the cursor location.

Or, you can specify a line number in the current file after which you want vi to read in a second file.

This is a great way to put two files together in preparation for sorting. Or, you can use this technique to assemble the parts of a collaboratively written report. You can even do some rudimentary mail-merging, as explained in the next section.

Mail Merge *vi* Style

You are drafting a series of letters—maybe about 10. With such a small number, you don't need a sophisticated electronic means of recording them; your Rolodex works just fine. You could write all 10 letters manually with your word processor, or even with your typewriter, but for some perfectly legitimate reason you have decided to do the work with **vi**. You do not yet know how to write a shell script to do the work for you, so you apply a little elbow grease to execute the following series of steps.

1. Create the letter in a file called form.letter. Include the salutation (Dear Friends:) and the closing (Sincerely,).

2. Create a return address and date in a file called from.txt.

3. Type **vi letter1** to open a new file for the first of your 10 letters.

4. Use Esc-**:** to get to the command line.

5. On the command line, type:

```
r from.txt
```

6. Refer to your Rolodex and type the first person's name and address. Remember to take advantage of the awesome **vi** commands you learned in Chapter 10. Use **i** or **a** to get into input or append mode, **o** to open up a new line below the current one, **O** to open a line above the current one, and so on.

7. Eyeball how the letter looks so far, and calculate how many lines you've used—maybe about 12? Or, if precision is your game, go to the command line (Esc-**:**) and type **set nu** to turn line numbers on. Then you'll know for sure how much space you need.

8. Get to the command line again, with Esc-**:.**

9. Type **14r form.letter** to retrieve the main part of the letter and start it at line 14 of the file.

10. Type **wq** on the command line to file the letter.

11. Move to the next person's address in your Rolodex, and start over again with **vi letter2**.

When you've finished typing all of the letters, print them in one fell swoop by typing:

```
lpr letter*
```

Before printing them, however, you should probably type **ls letter*** to make sure that you don't have any other files that start with the word *letter*.

CHAPTER 12

Somewhere around a Dozen Useful vi Commands

IN A NUTSHELL

- ▼ The / Command
- ▼ The // Command
- ▼ The :set nu Command
- ▼ The nG Command
- ▼ The :set nonu Command
- ▼ The J Command
- ▼ The ndd Command
- ▼ The ndw Command
- ▼ The 0 (zero) Command
- ▼ The nw Command
- ▼ The nb Command
- ▼ The n) Command
- ▼ The n(Command

All of the commands in this chapter are executed while you are in command or edit mode. That means, of course, that you must press Esc before you can make any of these commands work. If you're in input mode when you try them, you just type them into your text. No big deal. Use x, dw, r, or R to get rid of them.

The other thing to remember about vi is that upper- and lowercase letters are different. Sometimes the results may not be what you expected, if you mix up your cases.

Now try a few more cool vi commands.

The / Command

The / command searches for a string of characters. Say, for example, that you want to find the word *sharp* in a file on which you're working. Get into edit mode by pressing Esc. Type the slash (/) character to move to the command line. Then type the word you're looking for—in this case, it's *sharp*—and press Enter. Just like that, vi takes you to the next instance of the word *sharp*.

The // Command

The // command repeats the last search.

The :set nu Command

This command numbers the lines in the file. This is useful when you're editing long files.

To type any **set** command, get to the command line by typing Esc -:. Then type **set** followed by the desired attribute. You can set nu, nonu, or wm as described below. Or, since UNIXland is ripe with commands and options, you can undoubtedly set other attributes. These three are enough for now.

The *n*G Command

This command takes you to the line number specified by *n*. For example, to go to line number 100 of the file, type **100G**. It's not necessary to **set** nu to use the *n*G command—your lines have numbers, whether or not you can see them.

The :set nonu Command

This command turns off line numbers.

The J Command

The J command joins two lines. To use this command, press Esc to make sure you're in edit mode. Put your cursor anywhere within a short line. Type J to join the next line with the current line. If the current line is now too long, move your cursor to the beginning of a word near the end of the line, type i for input, and press Enter to move the rest of the line down.

"I HATE THIS!"

vi doesn't word-wrap!

I bet more people would use vi if they could figure out how to make it word-wrap! You know what *word-wrap* is. It's when your word processor moves the whole word to the next line if it doesn't fit on the current line. It's a cool trick that lets you keep on typing and typing and typing without ever hitting Enter, until your fingers fall off or you get to a new paragraph, whichever comes first.

OK. You can make vi at least *try* to word-wrap like your word processor does. Here's the intuitive (NOT!!) little trick:

Get to the command line by pressing Esc.

Type `:set wm=`*some number like 6*

What do you suppose wm stands for? Try *wrap margin!* To use this setting, you have to add text to your file using the a or A command (short for *append*), rather than i for input.

The *n*dd Command

If dd deletes a single line, what do you suppose 6dd does? Sure—it deletes the current line (the line that the cursor is positioned on) plus the next five lines, for a total of six.

The *n*dw Command

Ditto: If dw deletes a word, then, logically (at least, by vi logic), 2dw deletes two words—the current one and the one following it.

The O (zero) Command

The 0 command takes you to the beginning of the current line. In the same way that a big goose-egg is the opposite of the wad of dollars you used to have when you were single, so the zero in vi is the opposite of the dollar sign command, which, you recall, takes you to the end of the current line.

The *n*w Command

This command moves you forward the specified number of words. A w by itself moves you forward one word, whereas 6w moves you forward six words.

The *n*b Command

This command moves you backward the specified number of words. A **b** by itself moves you backward one word, whereas **6b** moves you backward six words.

The *n*) Command

This command moves you forward the specified number of sentences. A **)** by itself moves you forward one sentence, whereas **2)** moves you forward two sentences.

The *n*(Command

This command moves you backward the specified number of sentences. A **(** by itself moves you backward one sentence, whereas **4(** moves you backward four sentences.

There are lots of other vi commands. Someday someone should write a book about them all. But I'll bet you've had enough of this vi stuff and are ready to move on to something you can really sink your teeth into!

Next stop, file permissions. Hold on to your seats!

PART IV

Private and Public Information: Permissions

Includes:

CHAPTER 13

Mother May I? Permissions and How They Work

IN A NUTSHELL

▼ Getting permission information

▼ Interpreting the permission information you find

CHAPTER 13

Because UNIX systems often have both local and international network access, your files can, in theory at least, be accessed by anyone who has the proper login id and password or a criminal-enough mind to seek out your files. Most potential pilferers would have to go out of their way to access your files, but if they wanted to badly enough, they could probably do it. **You** already have enough UNIX knowledge to locate and read any files on your colleagues' accounts; you will gain still more knowledge of that type by the time you have finished reading this book. Scary, isn't it? Or maybe you're one of those "criminal" types, and you're already thinking, "Yesssssssssssssssssssss! Take me to the robbing and pillaging pages!"

There are at least a handful of factors that safeguard your files and keep you from facing outcomes ranging from embarrassment to certain doom.

Don't lose any sleep—no one cares about your files

✔ Your files are not that important. You aren't solely responsible for secure financial, military, or government data, are you?

✔ If you *are* responsible for secure financial, military, or government data, surely someone on your payroll is spending all of his or her time worrying about the security of your system, so you don't have to.

✔ Your files are not that interesting. Unless you have been spending your lunch hours writing love letters, manifestoes castigating your boss, or true confession novels, believe me, no one cares.

✔ Hardly anyone knows how to get to your files, nor what to do with them if and when they do manage to get to them. That's because they haven't read this book cover to cover as you are doing. You are to be commended for your unbelievable tenacity and for your unfaltering interest in something as inexcusably geeky as UNIX.

✔ The people who do know how to get to your files are much too busy to bother. They have bigger fish to fry.

So your files are safe. Skip the next two chapters. (NOT!)

You have to understand file and directory permissions so that, when you do create a file worth prying into, you can protect it. This chapter explains what file permissions are and how to find and use file permission information. In Chapter 14, you learn how to use file permissions to safeguard your files.

Listing Files To Reveal Permission Information

You are probably beginning to believe—quite rightly so—that the `ls` command is one of the most important commands in UNIXland.

The Newbies' Top 10 UNIX Commands

10. `ls`—list files

9. `mv` *oldfile newfile*—move a file or directory to a different location, or rename a file or directory

8. `rm` *filename*—remove a file

7. `man` *commandname*—bring up the manual (on-line documentation) for a particular command

6. `cd` *directoryname*—change to a different directory

5. `cp` *oldfile newfile*—copy a file

continues

The Newbies' Top 10 UNIX Commands (continued)

4. `mkdir directoryname`—create a directory

3. `rmdir directoryname`—remove a directory (only when all of the files inside it have been removed)

2. `passwd`—changes your password (about once a month, please!)

1. `logout, exit,` or `Ctrl-d`—depending on the kind of computer you have, one of these commands gets you out of UNIXland, back to reality!

To list your files, complete with permission information, type the following:

```
ls -l
```

If the `ls -l` command doesn't display group information for you, try `ls -lg`.

TIP

If you want to see all the files, including those that begin with a period (such as .login, .cshrc), add the a option to the `ls -l` command. It looks like this:

```
ls -la
```

The output of `ls -l` looks something like this.

```
total 4
drwxr-xr-x    2 kitalong    staff    512    Nov  10  14:22   Documents
-rw-r--r--    1 kitalong    staff    272    Nov  18   8:05   mail.data
-rw-r--r--    1 kitalong    staff    536    Dec   5  19:02   report.4.char
-rw-r--r--    1 kitalong    staff    138    Dec  14  14:53   sales.data
```

There was a list like this one back in Chapter 8, and an explanation about what each field means. This chapter concentrates on the first, third, and fourth fields of the display.

Interpreting Permission Information

Although this chapter concentrates on the first, third, and fourth fields in the display, I won't explain them in that order, because a "third-fourth-first" order makes more sense. The owner and group (third and fourth fields) information helps you understand how the first field works.

The Third Field: Owner

This is an easy concept to master. The owner is the person who created the file. You can remember this, because the owner field contains a login id, which, in most cases, is recognizable as someone you know—probably you!

I HATE UNIX!

The only leeettle weirdness is that in UNIX commands related to file permissions, the *owner* is often referred to as the *user*.

"I HATE THIS!"

Am I the owner or the user?!

For the purpose of identifying and changing file permissions, UNIX calls the owner of a file the *user*. This is to distinguish him or her from the world, which UNIX calls *other*. Since *owner* and *other* both start with *o*, UNIX felt compelled to pick a name for one of them that starts with a different letter of the alphabet. This was done without the aid of a thesaurus.

In this book, we have frequent lapses and unwittingly use the more logical names, owner and world. But since the commands you need to change permissions rely on knowing the goofy terminology, we feel a need to give you time to practice.

So, all together now,

"User, not owner. User, not owner."

"Other, not world. Other, not world."

Sheesh!! At least UNIX, in its infinite wisdom, didn't change the name of *group* to something like *organization*, and then designate its code as uppercase *O*. We have some small things to be thankful for in UNIXland.

The Fourth Field: Group Information

UNIX doesn't allow you, or even your system administrator, to exclude particular people from getting access to your files. That is, there is no UNIX command that says, "Anyone except Dorothy can read the files in my directory." If you want to exclude Dorothy, you have to exclude everyone else, too.

However, UNIX does allow you to set up groups and arrange for only the members of the group to have access. So, figure out a way to get Dorothy assigned to a different group and you're on your way. See Chapter 14 for more on defining and setting up groups.

In the preceding example, kitalong is a member of the group called "staff." If she wanted to, she could protect the files she owns by denying read, write, or execute (rwx) permission to everyone in the world (other) field, but allow rwx permissions to the members of her group.

Sample uses of group permissions

✔ In academic departments, set up a facstaff group so that students are denied access to grades and other sensitive records, while allowing faculty and secretaries to share such records. Set up another group to which the department's secretaries and administrators belong, but not faculty or students. This allows administrative staff to share certain departmental records without opening them up to faculty or students.

✔ In a corporation, create separate groups for marketing, research, administration, sales, personnel, finance, production, and any other departments that exist. Files in progress can then be shared among the members of each group before they are made public. Likewise, files that are of interest only to the members of those departments can be restricted.

continues

I HATE UNIX!

✔ In a financial services organization, maintain close group control over detailed revenue, expenditure, and payroll data and over individual customer accounts, while revealing up-to-date summary budget data to stockholders and anyone else who is interested.

The First Field: Permission Information

Believe it or not, the alphabet-soup left field in the `ls -lg` display is the key to understanding who has permission to do what to your files. You have learned that there are three classes of people for whom file access is allowed: the owner (or user, in UNIX parlance), the group to which the owner belongs, and all others (everyone in the world). There are also three classifications of permission: read, write, and execute.

HUH?

BUZZWORDS

LEVELS OF PERMISSION

Read permission (r) means that members of the designated classification—owner (user), group, or world (other)—can look at the file and copy it.

Write permission (w) means that a member of the particular classification is authorized to make changes to the file.

Execute permission (x) refers to directories and to executable program files. If you grant execute permission to a directory, people in the authorized classification have permission to `cd` to the directory. If you grant execute permission to a program file, people in the authorized user classification have permission to run the program.

Here are the permissions for two of the files listed in the above example. The first file is a directory named Documents. The second is a file named mail.data.

```
drwxr-xr-x   2 kitalong   staff   512   Nov 10 14:22   Documents
-rw-r--r--   1 kitalong   staff   272   Nov 18  8:05   mail.data
```

The 10-character first field can be broken up into four "zones," as shown in the following figure.

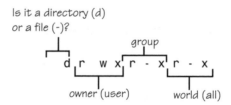

The first zone (labeled Identifier in the table) consists of a single character, either the letter *d* or a hyphen. This zone reveals that mail.data is a file, rather than a directory, because the zone contains a hyphen. In contrast, Documents is a directory, indicated by the letter *d* in that first zone.

Now, let's turn our attention to the part of the table labeled Permissions. Three zones are present in this section of the table. Each zone consists of a group of three characters.

The second zone tells us what kind of access the owner has. For the directory named Documents, the owner rightfully has read, write, and execute permission. For the file named mail.data, execute access is not needed, because mail.data is neither a program nor a directory. Almost without exception, the owner wants full permissions on all files that he or she owns.

Quiz: Can you think of an instance when, as the owner of a file, you might want to restrict your own write access to that file?

Answer: Perhaps you worked very hard to write a crucial program or to create a data file containing very specific information that must not be updated. Denying yourself write access ensures that you cannot change the file without taking an extra step, thereby forcing you to think carefully about the consequences of your actions.

The next zone, or group of three characters, indicates that members of the owner's group (staff) lack write access to these two files. They may read the mail.data file, and they may cd into the Documents directory. Files within the Documents directory may have different sets of permissions that need not be related to the permissions assigned to the directory.

Finally, the third and last zone, or group of three characters, indicates that "the world"—anyone who can access the UNIX system on which this file lives—can look at the contents of the file, and can cd to the directory, but cannot move or make changes to either. In short, the owner is comfortable with anyone else in the world looking at either the file or the directory, but wisely wants to reserve for herself the right to make changes.

Remember, read access to a file includes permission to copy that file to your own file system. You learned about copying files in Chapter 8.

I HATE UNIX!

CAUTION

The ease with which files can be transferred around the Internet calls into question the inviolability of copyright. The legal system is still trying to catch up with the new technologies. Stay tuned to your local news source for continuing attempts to protect copyright holders.

Don't fret about file permissions. In this chapter, you've learned how they work. In the next chapter, you learn how to manipulate and change permissions. Armed with these two practical concepts, you can safeguard files when necessary, and forget about permissions the rest of the time.

CHAPTER 14

Controlling Access to Your Files

IN A NUTSHELL

▼ Changing ownership
▼ Changing permissions
▼ Defining and changing groups

f Chapter 13 made you paranoid about the security of your files, this chapter is for you. Here's where you learn how to keep friends and fiends alike from tiptoeing in where they're not wanted. And, if you get so paranoid that you want to give away all your files rather than risk having them stolen, you learn how to change ownership, as well. In fact, let's begin with that.

Changing Ownership

The chown (change owner) command lets you give away files that you own. The syntax looks like this:

```
chown filename new_owner
```

For example, here is a file listing from Jim Longacre's home directory.

```
-rw-r--r-- 1 longacre staff 138 Jan 14 11:02 sales.data
```

Jim just got transferred from the sales force to the main office, and he wants to pass along his sales.data file to his successor, Debra Connors (dconnors). Here's the command:

```
chown sales.data dconnors
```

Now, when Debra needs to move the file into her own home directory, she won't have any trouble getting the proper access, because she's the rightful owner.

Changing Permissions

The basic command for changing permissions is chmod, short for change mode. Whereas you relinquish ownership of a file with chown, chmod is a less drastic move.

"I HATE THIS!"

How the heck do you pronounce chmod?

chmod can be sung to the tune of "Shh-Boom," that old fifties song. "chmod, chmod, owner-group-w-w-w-world." Repeat forever. You'll never get this tune out of your subconscious again!

OK, so everyone doesn't pronounce it sh-boom… er, I mean sh-mod. I once heard a lady on a TV show pronounce it like that, though, and I haven't been the same since. Just say the whole thing—change mode.

There are two ways to change file permissions, or modes, in UNIXland. The easy way uses letters of the alphabet. The complicated way uses numbers.

The Easy Way

The chmod command syntax is as follows:

```
chmod user_class action permission filename
```

There is a limited number of things you can type for *user_class*, *action*, and *permission*. Here are your options:

user_class	u, g or o
action	+ or -
permission	r, w, or x

Now, let's see how this works by looking at Debra Connors' sales.data file again.

```
-rw-r--r--  1 connors staff 138 Jan 14 11:02  sales.data
```

If Debra wants the members of her immediate group to be able to write to the file, but wants to restrict anyone else from even reading it, she would type:

```
chmod g+w o-r sales.data
```

The command means, "Change the group's (g) permissions by adding (+) write (w) permission. Change everyone else's permissions (o for other) by removing (-) read (r) permission. Perform these actions on the file named sales.data.

Now, if Debra types ls -l sales.data, she sees the following:

```
-rw-rw----  1 connors staff 138 Jan 14 11:02  sales.data
```

The problem is that everyone who works for the company is a member of the group called staff. To restrict access to certain files to the sales group, Debra will have to ask the system administrator to create a new group called sales. Then she can change the group ownership of her sales.data file. See the section titled "Changing Group Membership," later in this chapter for details.

Let's look at a couple more examples, just to make sure you're good and confused before we go on to the numeric method of changing file modes, which will confuse you permanently.

Sometimes people like to facilitate file sharing. Such folks may set up a special directory that grants read, write, and execute permission to anyone in the world, so that anyone who knows that directory is there can deposit files into it, and can grab copies of files that they find there. Such a directory might be called Incoming. Some people call it RJE (short for Remote Job Entry).

```
ls -l Incoming
drwxrwxrwx  1 kitalong staff 138  Apr 22 19:00 Incoming
```

Let's remove some of those permissions temporarily.

```
chmod u-w g-rwx o-rwx Incoming
```

Here's what the resulting permissions looks like when you issue the `ls -l` command.

```
dr-x------  1 kitalong staff 138  Apr 22 19:00 Incoming
```

What's wrong with this picture? The owner of the file removed write permission from herself as well as from everyone else! That won't do.

```
chmod u+w Incoming
```

There, that's better. The `ls -l Incoming` command now reveals:

```
drwx------ 1 kitalong staff 138  Apr  22 19:00 Incoming
```

But it's not much of an incoming directory without everyone having the proper access.

```
chmod g+rwx o+rwx Incoming
```

Clear as mud? If not, maybe you're a number person.

The Confusing Way: For Experts Only

If you can deal with numbers better than with letters and pluses and minuses, perhaps the numeric (or octal, for you UNIX purists) representation of file permissions works better for you. Here's how it works.

Each permission has a numerical value attached to it, as shown in the following table:

	read	write	execute
0		-	-
1	-	-	1
2	-	2	-
3	-	2	1
4	4	-	-
5	4	-	1
6	4	2	-
7	4	2	1

If you don't want to memorize a table, think about it this way:

> read permission   4
>
> write permission   2
>
> execute permission   1

The highest possible permission number is 7 for any user classification. An example probably helps at this point.

If, for a program named chart, you granted read, write, and execute permission to yourself, everyone in your group, and everyone in the whole wide world, the resulting ls -l output looks like this:

```
-rwxrwxrwx  1 kitalong  staff  138  Jun 19 14:20  chart
```

The octal code for the file's permissions is 777, because each user classification has full permission to act on the file.

To change it so that the group and world have read and execute permission, but not write permission, the command looks like this:

```
chmod 755 chart
```

Read permission (4) plus execute permission (1) equals 5.

The following directory has a permission code of 700 (read, write, and execute for the owner, no permissions at all for the group and the world).

```
drwx------ 1 kitalong    staff   138   Apr  22  19:00  Personnel
```

To retain the same permissions for the owner, add read and execute permissions for the group, and grant no permissions for the world, type:

```
chmod 750 Personnel
```

After you have internalized the table, or at least the codes for each permission level, this version of chmod is pretty easy, but some of us don't do well with numbers. If you understand octal codes, however, the next section is clearer.

Unmasking *umask*

The default umask on most UNIX systems is 022. Using the table presented in the previous section, we can interpret this number. It means, "Withhold no (0) permissions from the owner/user, and withhold write (2) permission from the group and the world."

UMASK

The *umask* is a file-creation mask that determines which permissions are withheld from different classes of users. The *umask* is attached to your account, so that every time you create a file or directory, the *umask* governs how the initial permissions should be set.

If you don't like your default *umask* (which is probably 022), you can change it. For example, to give full permission to everyone on all files you create from now until you log out, type:

```
umask 000
```

That is, withhold no permissions from anyone.

I HATE UNIX!

"I HATE THIS!"

Why on earth does *umask* use the opposite principle from *chmod*?

Why can't we just add up the permissions to be granted, instead of concentrating on the permissions to be withheld?

I really hate it when UNIX has a logical explanation for such frustrations. Here it is. If UNIX relied on the total number of permissions granted, the number would vary depending on whether the file in question is a plain data file, a program, or a directory. (Full permission on a program or directory is 777, while full permission on a plain data file is 666.)

By setting a *umask* to withhold partial permission, UNIX only has to tell each file one thing, regardless of what kind of a file it is.

To maintain the utmost security on your files—that is, to give yourself full permission but withhold all permissions from everyone else in your group and the world—type:

```
umask 077
```

If you want to change your default *umask* permanently, you have to put the appropriate command in your initialization file. See Chapter 18 on customizing your UNIX environment.

Defining and Changing Groups

Your system administrator is the only person who can set up a group, but once it's set up, you can change the group identity of any files you own, as long as you are a member of the group to which affiliation is being assigned.

This is a good time for an example. Remember that file that Debra Connors took possession of, a few pages back? We left it looking like this:

```
-rw-rw---- 1 connors staff 138 Jan 14 11:02  sales.data
```

The group id is staff. Debra wants to set up a special group called "sales" to which all of the members of the sales staff automatically belong. She talks to the system administrator, gets the group set up, and has the system administrator assign all 10 of the sales staff to that group.

Now, she can use the chgrp command to change the group affiliation of any files to which she wants her sales staff to have primary access. The syntax for the chgrp command is

```
chgrp group filename
```

So to change the group for the file sales.data, which, of course, she owns, Debra types:

```
chgrp sales sales.data
```

If you belong to more than one group, such as staff and sales, the system administrator assigns a primary group id (probably staff), and other subsidiary group ids. To display your group affiliation(s), use the id command. It displays your userid, as well as all of your group affiliations.

Now that you've learned the basics of your UNIX system, it's time to experience the wider world beyond your own immediate network. The next several chapters take you on a whirlwind tour of the Internet. You are about to experience e-mailing, followed by a smattering of data surfing, also known as cruising the Information Highway. Put on your water wings or fasten your seat belt, depending on which metaphor you prefer!

PART V

Electronic Mail

Includes:

CHAPTER 15
Communicating via E-Mail

IN A NUTSHELL

- ▼ E-mail basics
- ▼ How to get started
- ▼ The UNIX mail program
- ▼ Your first message
- ▼ Receiving mail
- ▼ Replying to messages
- ▼ Saving messages
- ▼ Forwarding messages
- ▼ E-mail etiquette

This chapter introduces you to the basics of electronic mail, or e-mail for short. If your UNIX system has e-mail capability, I'd be willing to bet that this will be one—perhaps the only—part of UNIX that you like. Of course, e-mail is not just available in UNIXland; most networks have some sort of electronic mail system.

E-Mail Basics

E-mail reaches your computer mailbox, whether or not you are logged in. In this respect, e-mail resembles snail mail.

ELECTRONIC MAIL, or E-MAIL

Electronic mail (e-mail) consists of messages sent by computer from one person to another. For e-mail to work, your computer must be connected, either directly via some kind of cabling, or indirectly, via a modem and phone lines, to a network of some sort, preferably a wide-area network (WAN).

SNAIL MAIL

Snail mail is the postal service mail. Computer aficionados gave it this somewhat derogatory name because of its agonizing slowness. Even if you've never used e-mail, the postal service seems slow. Once you've tried e-mail, anything sent through the postal service seems to have been sent on the back of a snail.

What's So Great about E-Mail?

Like most technological advances, e-mail has both advantages and disadvantages. Many of its attributes can be both advantages and disadvantages at the same time!

Like the little girl who had a little curl right in the middle of her forehead, e-mail, when it is good, is very, very good, but when it is bad, it can be horrid. Here are a few examples.

E-mail: Is it good or evil?

✔ *E-mail is an incredibly fast means of sending messages.*

Good: You can quickly disseminate information to and receive information from colleagues, subordinates, and people who share your interests. This communication covers thousands of miles in moments. Messages can be sent to an individual, or can be simultaneously sent to thousands of people.

Bad: You can communicate idiotic or erroneous information almost instantly over thousands of miles to one or many people. This can have the effect of making you look like a fool, or of getting you fired, depending upon the seriousness of the communication and the degree of idiocy you conferred on it.

✔ *E-mail is received even when the recipient is not logged in.*

Good: You can send messages at your convenience, and the recipient can read them at his or her convenience. Crossing time zones doesn't have to mean altering your sleep schedule or waking someone up with a phone call in the middle of the night.

continues

E-mail: Is it good or evil? (continued)

Bad: If, for some reason, the recipient doesn't read his or her e-mail regularly, there will be a serious delay (for example, the recipient may never read your message). Make sure the person is e-mail ready before you begin to rely on this means of communication.

✔ *Because e-mail messages reveal few social cues, like age, gender, race, or position in the company, people from all walks of life can communicate as equals.*

Good: Free exchange of ideas is fostered among people who rarely come into contact in their normal routines. The shop foreman can communicate with the president, the chair of the board of directors with a member of the word-processing pool. Problems are aired and innovative solutions can result.

Bad: Because e-mail is an evolving medium, the conventions are not well established. People may not understand how (or whether) traditional communication conventions translate into conventions for electronic media. Be careful.

✔ *Like postal service mail, e-mail can include pictures (digitized graphics), newspaper clippings (articles that have been typed or scanned into the computer), and formatted files, such as those produced by word processing programs and desktop publishing systems.*

Good: You can exchange all different kinds of information via e-mail, just as you can by way of snail mail. This process is deceptively easy, given the proper encoding/decoding software.

Bad: You shouldn't include digitized or encoded material in an e-mail message unless you are *very sure* that the person to whom you are sending the information has the software and wetware (brains, intelligence) to be able to decode and use the files you send.

Unless the digitized file is very important to the person, they probably will not go out of their way to figure out how to use it, unless they are already familiar with the appropriate software. Just because exchanging such files is common and simple to do within your company, you cannot necessarily assume that your correspondents outside the company have a similar set-up for encoding and decoding digitized information.

What You Need To Get Started

The best way to determine your e-mail requirements is to ask yourself a few questions. But don't stop there—answer the questions, too!

Not long ago, e-mail access was available primarily through educational institutions and large companies with deep pockets. Today, however, individuals and small businesses can take advantage of e-mail at prices that won't break the budget.

Major telephone companies, such as MCI and Sprint, offer e-mail options. CompuServe and Prodigy are commercial data services that include e-mail in their service menus. Direct access to the Internet is available both to commercial and to non-profit agencies, while BITNET (aka NREN) is available primarily to educational and research institutions. Other common and widely used networks include Fidonet and UUCP. Which one you choose depends largely on your needs and how much you are willing to pay.

I HATE UNIX!

✔ With whom will you exchange e-mail? Will in-house e-mail suffice? Or do you need to contact people outside the company, such as vendors, government agencies, contract employees, and the like?

✔ What capabilities will you need, beyond the basic half-dozen that all e-mail systems come with? Do you need audio transmission capability? What information encoding/decoding needs will you have? What kind of access will your employees need? Will they access e-mail only from their desks, or will they need to get to it while they are on the road?

✔ Which is more important, a uniform, easy-to-use interface that will work well on one or two hardware platforms, or a more general system that works on a variety of hardware, including over a modem?

✔ In what way(s) can you potentially gain access to a wide-area network such as the Internet?

✔ How much will this access cost you?

Currently available e-mail systems are too numerous to mention here. But they fall into two basic categories:

✔ GUI mail systems, such as MailTool, Xmail, or Eudora. These are menu-driven, point-and-click mail systems that have the advantage of being easy-to-learn and intuitive to use, but that don't easily work over modem lines or across platforms.

I HATE UNIX!

✔ Command-line mail systems, such as UNIX mail, Elm, and Pine, which require that you learn some commands, rather than allowing you to rely on visual cues from menus or buttons. The advantage of command-line mail systems is that they often can run on everything from a workstation to a dumb terminal to a PC connected via modem. Thus, they are very versatile.

Which type of e-mail system you choose depends on your needs and other constraints. Although the UNIX mail program is designed for people who are very comfortable in UNIXland—translation: it's kinda complicated—we use it as our example mail system, because it is a command-line e-mail program that is available on just about all UNIX systems. Even if nothing else is affordable, you can use UNIX mail.

How to buy technology

✔ Buy the most advanced system you can possibly afford. Don't buy something because it's cheap—if it's cheap, it's probably on the way out.

✔ Project your needs for at least three years and buy technology that does more than you think you need to do for the next three to five years.

✔ Buy technology that can be upgraded to the next generation.

✔ Don't take technological advancement personally. No matter how wisely or well you purchase, before you get your new toy out of the box, there is something better on the market. But if you wait for the latest and greatest, you will never buy, and you lose customers to your risk-taking competition.

Basic E-Mail Functions

The truth is that all mail systems perform the same basic functions.
Once you've mastered one e-mail system, all you have to do when faced
with a new e-mail system is figure out the specific way it handles those
basic functions.

Local Mail (Memos)

Many companies start out with an in-house e-mail system that resides on
a local-area network (LAN) and allows for exchange of messages and
files within the confines of the company. The best LAN-based system is
one that is connected to a wide-area network (WAN) so that e-mail can
be sent both in-house and around the world.

Messages sent on local-area networks can be compared to the in-house
paper memos that are so common in the business world. Your in-house
e-mail likely includes some messages that could (maybe *should*) have
been dealt with by a phone call—things like, "Where should we go for
lunch?" and "How much was the Jones Corporation's bid?" It is also
likely to include things like drafts of reports, letters, and budgets, which,
previously, may have been typed and circulated with a memo attached.

E-mail, especially in-house e-mail, may be either formal or informal. The
speed and spontaneity with which e-mail can be sent often makes it
seem as informal as a chat on the telephone. See "Emily Post Goes Electronic: E-mail Etiquette," later in this chapter, for e-mail good-behavior
guidelines.

Long-Distance Mail (Letters)

If you plan it correctly, you can use the same e-mail system for sending in-house and long-distance e-mail. In fact, you should look for a system that lets you expand from in-house to long-distance mail, and how readily you can expand the system should be one of the bases on which you evaluate an e-mail system.

Long-distance mail, that is, mail you send to people who don't work for the same company or department as you, might be a little more formal than in-house e-mail, in the same way that business letters are a little more formal than memos. But a lot depends on how well you know your correspondents, what kind of messages you send to them, and what your (and their) corporate culture is like.

Addressing Mail

The general format for e-mail addresses is id@node. The id part is the name the person uses to identify him- or herself to the computer system when they log in. Some ids we've encountered in this book include kitalong, dconnors, and samson. The @ sign means "at," and signifies that the next text is the name of a computer or site that's known by the network.

Some e-mail addresses are very long.

What makes an e-mail address longer than a freight train?

✔ The organization at which it is housed chooses to use very specific instructions to route the incoming mail to the exact machine on which the person's computer account resides. For example:
Joe_Blow@kokomo.indiana.org

✔ The network it is part of is not directly connected to other networks, so a very detailed (read: *convoluted*) addressing scheme is required. For example:
Plain_Jane%p6.f4.n9.z2.fidonet.org@spain.rain.com

TIP

Because e-mail is an evolving medium, with inconsistent address variations and a lot of people who are—believe it or not—less experienced than you are, you should make it your business to find out how your e-mail address works on different networks. Having e-mail does you no good if people can't reach you, and if they have to spend too much time figuring out how your e-mail address works, they may simply give up.

Using the UNIX Mail Program

When you make the leap to a UNIX system, electronic mail comes with your operating system. The program has an uninspired name — mail— and is a generic but very powerful e-mail system that lets you easily do anything you could possibly want to do with electronic mail. It isn't pretty, though.

If you have access to any other e-mail system besides UNIX mail, use it. Command-line mail systems, like Elm and Pine, offer versatility similar to that of UNIX mail, but with better built-in user tools, making them

much easier to work with. Likewise, mailx, the X Windows System mail interface, provides some user friendliness. Perhaps better yet are GUI mail interfaces such as Mail Tool, which I've used under OpenWindows running on a Sun workstation. Any of these products are prettier than the plain UNIX mail program. However, prettiness has a price—although such products make e-mail a visual, point-and-click medium, they cost money, both to purchase the software and to support it.

In this book, you are introduced to electronic mail by learning how to use UNIX mail to do the basic functions that all e-mail systems make available.

TIP

> If your e-mail system is something other than UNIX mail, you might want to spend your time reading the manual for that system instead of reading the next few sections of this chapter. You can skip ahead to the section "Emily Post Goes Electronic: E-mail Etiquette."

Creating Your First Message (You have to send mail to get mail)

To use UNIX mail to send a message to someone, type the following command at the UNIX system prompt:

```
mail id@node
```

If you are sending mail within your company, you can probably omit the node. So, to send mail to your colleague, Ted Samson, who works with you in the same department, you can probably get away with typing:

```
mail samson
```

The Top 10 Things All E-Mail Lets You Do

10. Quickly and easily send an urgent and important message to an individual or a group of people.

9. Quickly, easily, and entirely by accident, send a dirty joke to the wrong individual or to a group of people.

8. Send unkind but accurate comments about the boss's looks to people who shouldn't know that you're even capable of *thinking* such things, let alone writing them down.

7. Read mail that other people have sent you.

6. Receive mail and forward it to other people.

5. Receive mail and forward it to other people with comments attached. ("Who does Jonesy think he is, delegating his dirty work to me? Give me a break!")

4. Reply to mail instantly, before you have had time to think about what to say.

3. Store mail messages so you can refer to them later.

2. Send mail messages that other people will store and use against you later.

1. Create "nicknames" or aliases so that you can refer to people by the names you usually call them, instead of by their long, involved e-mail addresses. (Wouldn't you rather send mail to "Stinky" than to 42smithj@lockjaw.com?)

However, to send mail to a person on a different network or at a different node, or site, you need to give more information. For example, to

send mail to a customer, Roger "Salty" Morton, who works at a company called DataLess, you would type:

    mail salty@dataless.com

To practice, send mail to yourself. Contrary to popular belief, this does not make you go blind. People e-mail themselves all the time.

When you press the Enter key after typing the `mail` *id@node* command, UNIX acts like it went to lunch—you won't see a prompt or nary a trace of life on the system. This is a good sign.

Just start typing your message, and press the Enter key when you get to the end of a line. Don't make the lines too wide—about eight words (40 or so characters) is good.

    % mail salty@dataless.com
    Thanks for sending the price quote. I'll
    be back in touch with you by the end of
    the week.
    Dana

When you've typed all you want to type, you can get out of mail and send the message by typing Control-d (press and hold the Control key and type the letter *d*), or by typing a period on a line by itself and pressing the Enter key. This brings you back to the UNIX system prompt, with the message safely on its way to Salty.

If you want to send a message to more than one person, the same command works. Use either a space or a comma to separate the ids of each person.

    mail samson dconnors

If you want to put a subject line into the header of your mail message—which is a very good idea—the easiest way is to add an option to the `mail` command. For example, if you wanted to send mail to salty@dataless.com with the subject line "Price quote received," you would type the following:

```
mail -s ''Price quote received.'' salty@dataless.com
Thanks for sending the price quote. I'll
be back in touch with you by the end of
the week.
Dana
```

Why subject lines are important

✔ Some people get a lot of e-mail. If they can't sort the wheat from the chaff by the subject lines, they get terribly annoyed.

✔ When you work with the same people on a variety of projects, good subject lines can help them determine which e-mail relates to which project. Both priority-setting and productivity are enhanced.

✔ Subject lines serve as advance organizers, setting the tone and the mood for reading the rest of the message.

✔ Subject lines serve as a one-line summary of the mail's contents.

If you always want UNIX mail to ask you for a subject, use `vi` to edit your .mailrc file. Include the following line:

```
set asksub
```

I HATE UNIX!

EXPERTS ONLY

What do those two- and three-letter node extensions mean?

As you work with e-mail and the other network services introduced in the next few chapters, you will notice that many Internet e-mail addresses end with a two- or three-letter code. The following tables help you decode those codes.

Three-letter codes refer to the type of organization that owns the computer address. These codes usually identify organizations headquartered in the U.S., although exceptions are possible.

com	Company or commercial organization
edu	Educational institution
gov	Government agency
mil	U.S. military agency
org	Organizations not affiliated with government, military, educational, or commercial concerns

Recently, country codes were added for countries outside the United States. Each country has an identifiable two-letter code. We don't have space to include all of them here, but here are some examples.

Australia	au
Austria	at
Canada	ca

continues

What do those two- and three-letter node extensions mean? (continued)

Fiji	fj
Finland	fi
Germany	de
Mexico	mx
Japan	jp
Palau	pw
Sweden	se
Turkey	tr

Note: Don't ask how these countries became part of the example list. Authors of books have some privileges, one being to decide what should be deemed interesting.

Possession of a country code doesn't necessarily mean that a country has easy access to the Internet. Many of the country codes are in place in anticipation of readily available Internet access. Right now, the most reliable e-mail access is in the wealthier Northern Hemisphere countries in North America, Europe, and parts of Asia, but this is rapidly changing.

Receiving Mail
(Bills, bills, bills—and a sweepstakes)

If you managed to drop your false modesty and send yourself an e-mail message, you should now have some mail to read! This is always very exciting. To read your mail, type:

```
mail
```

without adding an address. Your in-box is displayed on the screen and looks something like this:

```
N  1 salty@dataless.com Tue Dec 21  16:20    27/4456
Quote sent
N  2 dconnors@mycorp.com Wed Dec 22 11:49    78/2755
Report draft
N  3 kitalong@mtu.edu   Wed Dec 22  14:22    55/1141
Test message

?
```

What do the fields mean?

"I HATE THIS!"

The beginning of the message scrolled off the screen before I could read it!

If the message you are reading is longer than one screen, it scrolls by until the bottom of the file is reached. If you're lucky, it scrolls slowly enough for you to read. I have not been so lucky; consequently, I don't use the mail program very often!

Well, luckily, there's a way to fix this. Use **vi** to add the following line to your .mailrc file:

```
set PAGER=more
```

✔ The first field is a code describing the message. Possible codes include:

> N = A new message. This field can also contain other letters.

> U = The message was in the Inbox the last time you read your mail, but you didn't read it.

> D = The message has been marked for deletion.

> R = A message you have already read.

✔ The second field is the message number. This number is used to select messages to be acted upon. You mainly use it for reading and replying to messages.

✔ The third field is the e-mail name and address of the person who sent you the message. In a regular postal service message, this would be the return address on the person's letterhead.

✔ The fourth field is the date and time the message was sent. This is local to the sender's system, so it may reflect serious time zone anomalies.

✔ The fifth field is the number of lines/words in the file.

✔ The sixth field is the subject of the message.

✔ A question mark (?) is the prompt that is displayed when you are working within the mail program.

To read a message, type the number of the message you wish to read. The message appears on the screen.

Handling Your Messages

Here are some commands you can use to move through your Inbox list of e-mail headers.

Command	Action
d	Deletes the current message. Actually, marks it for deletion.
u	Undeletes the current message. Marks it with a U for undelete, thus giving you a chance to change your mind.
+	Reads the next message.
-	Reads the previous message.
user	Reads all messages from the specified user name, like dconnors@mycorp.com.

Replying to Mail (In re: Yours of the 23rd)

When you want to reply to a message, first type the number of the message. Type this at the ? prompt:

    r

UNIX mail automatically zeroes in on the return address (the From: field) of the letter to which you are replying and transforms it into the mailing address (the To: field) on your reply. Piece of cake.

The same subject line is also picked up, but the word "Re:" is placed before the beginning of the subject line to signify to the recipient that it is a reply, rather than a fresh message.

You then can just type the message and send it, as described earlier in this chapter.

EXPERTS ONLY

Another reason to learn *vi*—creating a signature file

If you've been on e-mail for any time, you have probably noticed that some people append what are called *signature* or *autograph* files to their e-mail messages. A signature or autograph file contains your full name and e-mail address. Optional things to include in signature files are your snail mail address, phone number, FAX number, a cute saying, and sometimes, some text artwork.

Here's a sample signature block:

```
=.=.=.=.=.=.=.=.=.=.=.=.=.=.=.=.=.=.=.=.=.=.=.=.=.=
Denise Jones                    jones@mycorp.com
1102 Cogsworth Rd
Plymouth, KY 00000          I try to take one day at a
(000)555-9908               time, but sometimes several
FAX (000)555-9999           attack me at once.
=.=.=.=.=.=.=.=.=.=.=.=.=.=.=.=.=.=.=.=.=.=.=.=.=.=
```

To create one of these masterpieces, use the vi editor, which you never thought you would need again. Name the file sign or Sign.

```
vi Sign
```

or

```
vi sign
```

You can have two signature files, if you wish. Use Sign for e-mail that goes outside the company and sign for internal messages. That way you can send a more elaborate and detailed signature file to people who don't know you very well.

Once you have created sign or Sign files, you can autograph your messages by typing ~a (for the sign file) or ~A (for the Sign file) on a new line in the mail file. Here's how Denise Jones would include her Sign file into an e-mail message to Ted Samson.

```
mail samson@mycorp.com
Subject: Lunch
Ted, Do you have time for lunch today?
I'd like to talk to you about the
Durfield contract.
~A
.
```

Remember the . by itself on a line quits and sends the message.

Saving Messages
(Don't deny it; I've got a copy of the e-mail)

You use the message numbers to save your mail messages. You can save a single message or a group of messages with one command.

```
save message-number filename
```

For example, if you wanted to save dconnors. Report draft in a file named deb.report in your home directory, type the following command at the mail (?) prompt:

```
save 2 deb.report
```

If you wanted to save two e-mail messages to the same file, type:

```
save 12 19 new_project
```

Saved mail messages are accessed by typing:

```
mail -f filename
```

For example, to read the saved mail message that contains Deb's report, type:

```
mail -f deb.report
```

Messages can also be accessed with vi. For example:

```
vi deb.report
```

Forwarding Mail
(Here, you take care of this)

Often, you want to delegate the answering of an e-mail message to someone else on your staff, or want to alert another person to an especially
interesting bit of information related to their work, hobbies, or love interest. The e-mail forwarding feature is perfect for this type of information exchange.

"I HATE THIS!"

Delegating work should be easy!

The UNIX mail forwarding feature is crummy. It's not as easy
to delegate work with UNIX mail as with other mail systems!!!

Here's what you have to do to forward something to someone:

Clean out your mailbox, either by saving or discarding all the messages
you have received, *except for the one you want to forward.*

Be sure to use the quit command to get out of mail, to ensure that everything you marked for deletion or saving is dealt with properly.

Now, the only thing left in your mailbox should be the message you
want to forward—let's say it's the one in the previous example that's
from salty@dataless.com, and you want to send it on to
darby@mycorp.com.

At the normal UNIX prompt, *not within mail,* type the mail command
with the -F option, which stands for "Forward."

```
mail -F darby@mycorp.com
```

EXPERTS ONLY

Using aliases or nicknames

If you don't like remembering long, convoluted e-mail messages, you can set up an alias (or nickname) file to help you keep track of people's addresses.

Aliases are placed in your .mailrc file. You have to use vi to access that file so type the following:

```
vi .mailrc
```

You can put the aliases anywhere in the file, but it's a good idea to keep them all together. Use the down arrow key to go to the bottom of the file. Then use the o command to open a new line below the last line.

If I wanted to be able to address Deb Connors as Deb instead of dconnors@mycorp.com, I would type the following on the new empty line I just created:

```
alias Deb dconnors@mycorp.com
```

Now, the next time you want to send mail to Deb, you can type:

```
mail Deb
```

Remember, the case is important in UNIX. So you'll have to type Deb with a capital D if that's how you type it in your alias file.

The mail program searches your .mailrc file for such an alias and then attaches the correct address to the message.

Another really important use for the **alias** command is to create mail groups. Let's say you want to create a group alias for all the people in the sales department. You include the following command in your .mailrc file:

```
group sales dconnors,rmorland,samson,lgrimley
```

To send mail to a group alias, type:

```
mail sales
```

The mail program searches your .mailrc file for the alias and routes the message to everyone in the group.

TIP

If you're a bit leery about editing your .mailrc file, because you remember that, earlier in this book, we issued an injunction against editing any file beginning with a period, you can protect yourself by making a copy of the original .mailrc file before you start messing around with it. Do this by typing the following:

```
cp .mailrc mailrc-old
```

Then, if you screw up, you can just delete the .mailrc file, and get the original one back by typing:

```
mv mailrc-old .mailrc
```

Exiting UNIX Mail

To get out of the mail program, you have two choices of commands to type at the ? prompt:

    Exit

or

    Xit

Typing either of these keeps your Inbox intact. Even mail marked for deleting or saving is retained in your mailbox.

If you type the following:

    Quit

it gets you out of the mail program and executes all of your desired commands (delete, save, undelete, etc.)

Emily Post Goes Electronic: E-Mail Etiquette

Because e-mail is alternately (or simultaneously) very, very good and quite horrid, some guidelines for this new medium do prevail.

Don't humiliate yourself when you use e-mail

✔ Never abuse or harass anyone via e-mail. Never send messages fraught with sexual, racial, religious, homophobic, or other bigoted language.

✔ Assume that anything you send electronically can become public. It is easy to store, forward, print, and otherwise publish electronic

communications. Someday, someone will distribute a message you sent, with or without your consent.

✔ Use language as clearly, accurately, concisely, and unambiguously as you can. There are several reasons for this. Because the recipient can't hear your tone of voice or read your body language, and may never have met you in person, the only thing they have to go on is what they read on-screen. Also, your spelling and grammar have to speak for you, so check them carefully.

✔ If you must use humor, especially sarcasm, use it sparingly. It's easy to misinterpret words read on a computer screen, without other cues. Also, in an increasingly global society, many of your readers may not be native speakers of your language, and may take your humor literally.

✔ Don't type in all uppercase text. Use mixed-case. There are two reasons for this, one related to readability and the other to network etiquette.

All uppercase text is difficult to read, because, believe it or not, people tend to use "word shapes" as a guide in understanding the meaning of a passage.

People on the networks often view all-caps as "shouting." You might get a negative reaction if you use all uppercase.

✔ Don't send special characters (like boldface, underline, italics, or other characters that you might create with special key combinations on your keyboard. Unless you are communicating with someone who has exactly the same e-mail system as you do, any special characters you try to send are at the very least, turned into gibberish on-screen. In some cases, such control characters are interpreted as commands by the recipient's e-mail system.

continues

Don't humiliate yourself when you use e-mail (continued)

✔ If your e-mail system doesn't automatically word wrap, avoid lines
longer than about 60 characters (8 to 10 words). Your recipients
will have an easier time reading your messages if the lines are relatively short.

CHAPTER 16

Internet Basics

IN A NUTSHELL

▼ What you need to get started
▼ Logging in to other computers with Telnet
▼ Transferring files with `ftp`
▼ For more information

I HATE UNIX!

The Internet is the world's largest computer network. Less than 10 years ago, the Internet was an arcane collection of data repositories used mainly by a few high-level or very specialized researchers. If you were on the Internet in those days, you might find data banks for particle physics, computer programming languages and operating systems, or military documents. The people who needed such data either were computing experts themselves, or worked with computing experts who could help them when they ran into trouble.

Today, the Internet is an easily accessible information resource for everyone. The data for computer scientists, particle physicists, and military personnel are still out there, but, in addition, you can find information of interest to runners, gardeners, biologists, technical communicators, and English literature professors. You can find data about Asian culture, art, philosophy, chemical engineering, Norwegian politics, or Texas barbecue. And if you can't find items of interest to you, you can start your own "Center for the Study and Appreciation of Yams" or "Medieval Armor Aficionado's Network."

All that information "out there" is available to you. To access it, all you need are two basic commands. Scary, isn't it?

Actually, some computers have special GUI software that makes it possible for you to access information on the Internet without ever typing a single command. For example, the Fetch program, which is available on Macintoshes, provides a visual interface for the ftp (file transfer program) command, enabling you to bring files and other information from other networked computers back to your computer.

Since all GUI programs are just facades that pretty up the bare-bones commands, just like the old false-front buildings used to pretty up the Old West towns, it's a good idea to learn to use the actual commands. Then, if you ever get a fancy GUI program to do your thinking for you, you'll feel like you've died and gone to heaven.

What You Need To Get Started on the Internet

You need very little to get started working with the Internet. Any computer, including an ancient IBM XT or a dumb terminal, lets you run the `telnet` and `ftp` commands, as long as you can make that computer connect somehow to a full-blown network machine like the one at your office that runs UNIX.

Are You on the Internet? How To Find Out

One way to find out if you are on the Internet is to log in to your UNIX computer and type one of these commands:

telnet

ftp

If these commands are not enabled, you will get an error message, something like, `Bad command or file name`. But don't give up yet. Try changing to the directory that stores programs on your system; perhaps with one of these commands:

```
cd /usr/bin
```

```
cd /usr/local
```

Use the `ls` command to check the contents of those directories. Who knows, you might find the `telnet` or `ftp` commands hidden away there.

Or you could use the `find` command, described in Chapter 8, to search the entire file system starting with the root. This, of course, would take a long time, but then you'd know for sure whether or not the commands are available to you!

Once you know where the `telnet` and `ftp` commands are hidden, it's just a matter of typing the whole command, path and all, such as

    /usr/bin/telnet

Eventually, you or your system administrator can set up the path so that you have direct access to the commands you need to explore the Internet.

If your `telnet` and `ftp` commands are successful (that is, the programs are available on your system), the system prompt will change to this:

    telnet>

or

    ftp>

Once you see such a prompt, you know that the commands are working. Now, type `quit` at either prompt, get back to your regular UNIX system prompt, and let's play ball.

Logging In To Other Computers (The host with the most)

To connect and log in to another computer, use the `telnet` command. You may already be familiar with this command if you run UNIX "remotely" from a networked PC, terminal, or other computer that doesn't itself run UNIX. The syntax for the `telnet` command is

    telnet computername [portname]

Occasionally, you have to specify a port name when you use the `telnet` command. If that is necessary, the instructions you are following should tell you so.

I HATE UNIX!

HUH?

BUZZWORDS

HOST

The computer to which you connect with the `telnet` command is sometimes called the *host*, because it welcomes you into its file system and gives you the run of the house. Therefore, do not overstay your welcome, nor go into any part of the home directory to which you have not been specifically invited. In short, stay out of non-public areas on host computers.

Questions to ask before Telnetting to a host computer

✔ *What login id should I use?*

You may be assigned a special, individualized login id. Or, if you're telnetting to a publicly accessible host, such as those in the examples provided later in this chapter, you may use a general login id that often reflects the name of the service you are accessing.

✔ *What password should I use?*

Some public Telnet hosts don't require a password. If they do, the password is provided along with the login id in the instructions for accessing the host. If you are granted an individual login id on a host computer, you'll need a login id and a password like the one you use when you log in to your UNIX account.

✔ *How can I find out about Telnet sites of interest to me?*

On-line information indexes are starting to crop up. But one of the best ways to find out about on-line information is still to listen and watch for it everywhere. For example, almost every month, I read about a new on-line service in one of my professional journals. I also hear about useful sites from colleagues, from e-mail, or from reading books and articles about the Internet. If you let your interests be known, people will start giving you the scoop. That kind of scoop tends to snowball!

NASA Spacelink

Here is a sample Telnet host that you might have a good time with—the NASA Spacelink site. To access it, type:

```
telnet spacelink.msfc.nasa.gov
```

For the NASA Spacelink site, the initial login is `newuser` and the initial password is also `newuser`.

When you have successfully entered the NASA site, you receive further on-screen instructions on how to obtain a permanent login id. You are also given the opportunity to explore the on-line data about the U.S. Space Program and about space exploration in general.

Federal Information Exchange

The Federal Information Exchange consolidates federal government information of interest to educators. To access it, type:

```
telnet fedix.fie.com
```

The login id is `new` the first time you use the system. To continue, you have to register with an id of your choice. No password is necessary. Read the on-line instructions on the first screen or two to get started.

Colorado Association of Research Libraries (CARL)

Now, let's see what the on-line library of the future might look like. Try telnetting to CARL, the Colorado Association of Research Libraries. Digital text, book reviews, and other items of interest are on line for your browsing pleasure. Use the following to access CARL:

```
telnet pac.carl.org
```

No login id or password is necessary.

I HATE UNIX!

The initial screen or two should give you enough information to go exploring. The main thing you have to remember is how to get out: At any screen, type //**exit**.

If you try the Telnet program a few times, and can't figure out what's so interesting about it, don't fret. Maybe it's not for you, or maybe you just haven't found that special something that gets you excited.

Keep in mind, though, that every day, someone, somewhere, puts information on the Internet. If there's nothing out there for you today, maybe tomorrow there will be. Already, some information is available only in electronic form. You place yourself at an advantage by getting some practice with the `telnet` command, so you can access that information when you need it.

Finally, Weather Information, Whether You Want It Or Not

You can access madlab, a menu-driven weather information service for the U.S. and Canada. Type:

```
telnet madlab.sprl.umich.edu 3000
```

Note: 3000 is a port number.

"I HATE THIS!"

The Internet can cause psychological problems

As I write this, our weather has bottomed out at –10 degrees Fahrenheit. The wind chill is –40. My husband is trying to thaw out his car. So far, he's tried a heat lamp, a space heater, and a magnetic oil-pan heater. Nothing has worked. The next tool on his list is a hair dryer, with which he successfully thawed the water pipes this morning.

continues

227

> ## The Internet can cause psychological problems (continued)
> Meanwhile, I just telnetted to madlab, where I learned that in Dallas it's 70 degrees Fahrenheit, with light winds. I am now severely depressed. Why don't they ever talk about the wind chill when it's warm outside? Maybe in Dallas, the wind chill is 63 degrees.

Transferring Files with *ftp*

File Transfer Program, or FTP, is a way of getting information from host computers back to your home computer. Unlike Telnet, which logs you in to the host computer, FTP merely connects you for the purpose of file transfer, rather like opening a spigot on both ends of a pipe, so that information can flow through it from one computer to another.

A lot of FTP-able information is housed on the Internet at "anonymous FTP sites." They are anonymous because the people who deposited the information there don't really care who accesses it, so they don't require individual login ids. Everyone just logs in as anonymous.

Here's what the syntax looks like:

```
ftp hostname
```

If you are prompted for a password enter your e-mail address.

There's no telling what file formats you'll find at an anonymous FTP site. However, the following commonly-used file extensions can give you a clue as to what kind of software it takes to read the file.

.ps PostScript file. To read, you must print it on a PostScript printer

.zip A compressed DOS archive of files. You need the `unzip` program to use this file. You must also transfer it as a binary file.

.txt AHHHH. This is a plain text file. You can look at it on-screen, using `vi` or `cat`.

.asc Ditto. No problem reading this one.

.doc Ditto. No problemo.

.Z A compressed UNIX file. Easy to deal with using the UNIX `uncompress` command, described later in this book.

.arc A compressed, archived file.

EXPERTS ONLY

Many files on Internet hosts are compressed in some way to save space. *Zipping* is just one compression type. There are others.

If you don't know how to uncompress files, begin by looking for files with an extension of .txt, .doc, or .asc. Eventually, when you find something that you need that is stored in a compressed, zipped, or binary format, you'll find a way to get it. Most of the software you need is available free of charge (via FTP) right there on the Internet.

Practice makes perfect, so let's try a couple of hosts.

PC Magazine

How about articles from *PC Magazine*? Many useful articles from back issues are accessible by typing:

```
ftp wuarchive.wustl.edu
```

Login as **anonymous** and type your login id as the password.

Wait, you're not out of the woods yet. FTP sites usually provide less initial information than Telnet sites do, and require that you enter a few UNIX commands to find precisely what you are looking for.

Start by typing `ls` to list the files in the initial directory. Or, if you want more information about the files, use the `dir` command, which gives you an `ls  -l`-like file listing. You can also type `pwd` to see where you are.

If you're not sure where to look for the information, you can just start `cd`-ing to directories at random. Sometimes the organization of the host's file system is pretty obvious, but in the *PC Magazine* archive case, it isn't. You can find the *PC Magazine* files by typing:

```
cd /mirrors/msdos/pcmag
```

Now `ls` the files to see what you can see. What you see is a whole long list of files, most of which end with the extension .arc or .zip. These extensions indicate that the files have been compressed, meaning that you need special software residing on your local computer to use the files. Fortunately, the `wuarchive.wustl.edu` site also houses at least the software needed to "unzip" zipped files—look a few directories above the pcmag directory to locate that software and drag (`get`) it back to your site, if you don't already have it.

Another thing you need to know about zipped files is that they are binary files, which means that you have to type an extra command to retrieve those files. So, before you retrieve any files, type:

binary

Now, whenever you find a file that looks interesting, use the get command to yank the file back through the pipe to your home directory. Here is the get command:

get *filename*

Be sure to type the file name exactly as it appears on the host, including uppercase and lowercase letters.

After a couple of seconds (maybe longer if the network is very busy or the file is very large, the file transfer is complete, and the file is stored in your home directory.

TIP

Using the ftp command indiscriminately is a really good way to quickly fill up your home directory. Don't forget to use your rm command to get rid of the practice files!

Space Shuttle Images

Let's try another one. There is an FTP site for space shuttle images. To access it, type:

ftp sseop.jsc.nasa.gov

Login with the anonymous id, as is customary for FTP sites, and give your login id if prompted for a password.

When you transfer image files, you have to recognize that they are binary files. What that means is that you must transfer them in binary mode. By default, FTP is in text mode. To switch to binary mode, type:

```
binary
```

Now you can use the `cd`, `ls`, and `pwd` commands to mosey around the Johnson Space Center, and the `get` *filename* command to bring back any image files that intrigue you.

You might have to do a little fooling around on your home system to view image files. Remember that computer science major who works at the deli across the street from your office? Well, this would be a good time to enlist his help if you can't get these files to print or show up on your screen. (Maybe you can feed him to repay him for his time—he'd probably welcome a meal that doesn't include corned beef on rye!)

To switch back to ASCII (text) mode after you have finished transferring binary files, type:

```
ascii
```

Project Gutenberg

Another FTP site that might be of interest is the Project Gutenberg site. A bunch of interested, unpaid people *scan* in copyright-free texts like *Alice in Wonderland*, *Peter Pan*, *Aesop's Fables*, Frederick Douglass's writings, and many others. Anyone who wants to own an electronic copy of any of these works is free to grab it by typing:

```
ftp mrcnext.cso.uiuc.edu
```

Login as `anonymous`. Go to the `etext` directory by typing:

```
cd etext
```

I HATE UNIX!

At the Project Gutenberg site, the index of all of the files begins with two zeroes. To double-check its name, type `ls 0*`

HUH?

BUZZWORDS

SCAN

A *scanner* is a device that allows a computer to read printed text and turn it into a file that can be stored electronically. The simplest scanners take a "snapshot" of the page and store it as a graphics file. More advanced scanners, such as those used by the Project Gutenberg volunteers, transmit text to the computer as though it had been typed on the keyboard. It is a huge job to scan large volumes of work, such as the Project Gutenberg documents. Each page of the book or article is read by the scanner, stored on the computer, and checked for accuracy. (Scanners make a lot of mistakes—for example, they often confuse letters that look alike, such as "i" and "l".

When you review the Project Gutenberg index file, notice that the files are sorted by the year they were entered. So you have to `cd` to the appropriate year's directory, then `get` the file you like.

For More Information

Both Telnet and FTP have many options and many more capabilities than are outlined here. If you want to explore these commands more thoroughly, you really ought to pick up a good book on the subject. You can get one free on the Internet! Here's how to get your very own copy of *Zen and the Art of the Internet*. Type:

`ftp ftp.cs.widener.edu` (yes, the host name begins with ftp!)

Login as anonymous and use your login id as a password. Next, cd to the pub/zen directory.

```
cd pub/zen
```

ls the contents of the pub/zen directory, to get a feel for what is there.

```
ls
```

The document is available in a variety of formats. Look for the format you want and get it.

```
get filename
```

Things to remember about FTP-ing

✔ Use anonymous as your login and your e-mail address (or login id) as your password.

✔ When you're FTP-ing, look for README, INDEX, or other files the names of which seem to indicate that they contain information about the site or its files. Then get those files and read them. You'll be surprised at what you might learn.

✔ Use normal UNIX commands—ls, cd, cd .., pwd, and who knows which others—to move around in an FTP site.

✔ Use the get command to bring files back to your home directory.

✔ Use the binary command to get compressed or archived files, graphics, word processing files, and other files that are not plain-vanilla ASCII files. Note, however, that .ps files act like ASCII files, so you don't need to switch modes to get them.

✔ When you're finished get-ting binary files, if you still want to get some other files, change modes back to ASCII by typing ascii.

Things to remember when you're Telnetting

✔ Read the first few screens carefully. Follow the instructions on those screens, and make a note of pertinent information.

✔ Many sites require that you register with a login id and perhaps a password. Keep track of those. The most high-tech method I've found is a small notebook that I keep next to my computer. An on-line file works too—yet another reason to use vi. Of course, whichever method you use to keep track of your Telnet ids and passwords should be kept secure. For that reason, the notebook-next-to-the-computer method is probably safer!

✔ As soon as you log in, always figure out the command for exiting the program. Sometimes it's easy to figure out, but sometimes it's not at all intuitive. Those first few screens probably contain a line or two about exiting, so don't fail to read them, and write the command down if necessary.

The most important thing to remember—whether you're using Telnet, FTP, or some other computer program—is to keep trying, even if you can't figure things out at first. It takes a bit of practice to become fluent on the Internet, but it is worth your while to develop some facility. The Information Superhighway is coming and you want to be in the fast lane.

Happy Internetting!

CHAPTER 17

Where To Find Information on the Internet

IN A NUTSHELL

▼ Using Gopher
▼ Reading on-line news
▼ Using Archie
▼ Commercial services

This chapter introduces you to other Internet tools besides Telnet and FTP. You visit Gopher, read news, Archie, and a few of the commercial services that are available. Not everything about these services is included here. All this chapter does is whet your appetite.

Gophering on the Internet (*Caddyshack revisited*)

Gopher, developed at the University of Minnesota (home of the Golden Gophers sports teams), is a menu-based Internet tool that lets you search out (go-fer) information. You select items of interest and move from site to site through a system of menus.

If you have a Gopher client program on your computer, you are able to get to it by typing:

```
gopher
```

at the UNIX prompt.

If the Gopher client program is there, you see a menu, something like the following:

```
Internet Gopher Information Client 2.0 pl10

Root gopher server: hafnhaf.micro.umn.edu

 —>    1.   Information About Gopher/
        2.   Computer Information/
        3.   Internet file server (ftp) sites/
        4.   Fun & Games/
        5.   Libraries/
        6.   Mailing Lists/
        7.   News/
        8.   Other Gopher and Information Servers/
        9.   Phone Books/
       10.   Search Gopher Titles at the University
             Minnesota <?>
       11.   Search lots of places at the U of M <?>
       12.   UofM Campus Information/
```

Another way to get to a particular Gopher server, if you have the Gopher software on your computer, is to type:

```
gopher hostname
```

For example, I often go(pher) to the Internet Film and Video Resource Library at the University of Michigan by typing:

```
gopher una.hh.lib.umich.edu
```

If you don't have a Gopher client, but you can telnet (see Chapter 16), you can telnet to a public Gopher client at another site. A popular one is at the University of Minnesota; the introductory Gopher menu shown previously is from Minnesota's Gopher. Use these commands:

```
telnet consultant.micro.umn.edu
login: gopher (no password is needed)
```

EXPERTS ONLY

If you don't have the Gopher software on your computer, you can get it free via anonymous FTP—or, better yet, have your system administrator obtain and install it for you. To get your own copy of the Gopher software, type the following commands at the UNIX prompt:

```
ftp boombox.micro.umn.edu
login (as anonymous)
password (type your e-mail id)
cd pub/gopher
get filename
```

Other sources are available for the Gopher software. You can use Archie, described later in this chapter, to find other sources.

How To Use Gopher

Once you have accessed Gopher, you can select menu items either by typing the number of the menu item or by using your arrow keys to scroll to the item you want and pressing the Enter key.

Each time you select an item from the menu, you see another menu, a file, or a searchable database. You can predict which.

How to predict where a Gopher menu item will lead

✔ If the menu item ends in a slash(/), selecting it makes another menu appear.

✔ If the menu item ends in a period(.), selecting it makes some kind of file appear.

✔ If the menu item has a <?> symbol after it, selecting it leads you to a searchable database, often a phone book or other directory.

Any Gopher server can be used to take you to other Gophers. Some-where, usually on the Gopher's initial menu, you see a selection labeled `Other Gopher and Information Servers` (number 8 on the Gopher menu shown previously). If you select that item, other Gopher servers are accessible from subsequent menus. At some level, you will probably see a menu item labeled `All the Gopher Servers in the World`, which is, indeed, just what it says it is!

Navigating within Gopher

Besides the numbered menu items, which let you travel around the Internet without necessarily knowing any commands other than `gopher`, Gopher clients are equipped with navigation menu selections, displayed across the bottom of your screen.

Depending on what it says on the bottom of the screen, there are five different things you can do with the items at the bottom of your Gopher screen:

u	Moves you up a screen, lets you walk backward through the screens you previously visited.
q	Quits Gopher. You are prompted to confirm that you really want to quit.
m	Mails the file to you or someone else and prompts you for an e-mail address, then sends the file to that address.
s	Saves the file in your home directory. You may be prompted for a filename, or given the opportunity to type a new file name if you want. Note, though, that if you have telnetted to the Gopher server, this selection won't work for you. You have to use e-mail!
Press <Return> to continue	Returns you to the menu from which you selected the item.

Your Personal Information Repository—On-line News

There's a program called rn (short for read news, but not to be confused with a similar program readnews) The rn program is available on most UNIX systems. It allows you to read Internet news on a mind-boggling span of topics.

The first time you use rn, it takes you a while to get it customized for your preferences. Don't start rn unless you have about an hour to go

through the various newsgroups and unsubscribe yourself from the ones you aren't interested in, or that, even if you were interested, you don't have the time to browse. When I did this, I found over 6,000 newsgroups! I could have spent the rest of my life reading! I got it down to about 120, still a large number, but not nearly as overwhelming as 6,000!

Once you've zeroed in on a manageable number of newsgroups to keep on top of, you will enjoy reviewing and responding every few days.

OK. To read on-line news, type:

```
rn
```

The first time you do this, go through the list to identify the groups you want to read. To get rid of the ones you don't want to read, type **u** to unsubscribe from that group.

"I HATE THIS!"

I have to unsubscribe from every group I don't like?!

That's like paying extra for sugar-free canned fruit, or paying to have my phone number unlisted. I should have to ask for what I want, rather than refusing what I don't want!

Well, if you didn't have to manually unsubscribe, how would you know what newsgroups are out there? The folks who put rn together were protecting your right to get as much information as is available; they have no way to know what information you want, and don't want to deny you anything.

I HATE UNIX!

EXPERTS ONLY

If you want to do the unsubscribing process manually—without going through the newsgroup files—do the following:

1. Run the **rn** command.

2. As soon as the program is loaded, quit rn by typing

   `q`

3. Edit the file .newsrc in your home directory. To do this, type:

   `vi .newsrc`

4. Notice that each line of the file ends with a colon. A colon means you are subscribed. If you want to unsubscribe from a group, change that colon to an exclamation point (!).

   You can do this one line at a time by positioning your cursor on the **:** and typing **r!** or you can do a global search and replace that will change all the colons to exclamation points. The command to do this is:

   `%s/:/!/`

   Next, go through each line of the file and subscribe to those groups you are interested in. To do this, position your cursor on the **!** at the end of the line, and type **r:** to replace the ! with a :. Now you are subscribed to only the groups you are interested in.

> **5.** When you have finished, get to the command line by pressing Esc followed by a colon, then type **wq** to write and quit the file.
>
> **6.** The next time you run **rn**, only the groups to which you subscribed are displayed.

The UNIX rn command has many options. The command to find all these options is

```
man rn
```

There are also other news reading programs. For instance, tin, another news reading program, acts a lot like rn, in that it is a character-based, rather than a GUI program. You may have a GUI-based news reader, which gives you point and click capabilities and menu-driven subscribing and unsubscribing. Check into it. It's worth your time.

Finding Information with Archie

Earlier in this chapter, you were introduced to Gopher, which helps you find all kinds of information on the Internet. The trouble with Gopher is that, although it's fun, it's somewhat random. Unless you know what you want and where it is stored, you will have trouble locating information in a systematic way.

Archie, on the other hand, provides a systematic way of searching for files, especially software, on the Internet. Archie is very easy to use, and just about any search turns up all kinds of sites through which your desires can be fulfilled (well, some of your desires!). An Archie keyword search turns up a list of files that match your keyword, and identifies

where those files are housed. Then, you can use FTP, or perhaps Gopher, to retrieve the materials.

There are a number of Archie servers around the world. To access Archie, you have to use Telnet to connect to one of the available servers (see Chapter 16 for information on using Telnet). Well- mannered Archie users connect to the Archie server that is geographically closest.

Archie Servers

Sometimes you can tell by the name of the server where it is located. Three common ones in North America are at Rutgers University, the University of Nevada at Las Vegas, and McGill University. Here are the Telnet addresses of the available Archie servers.

Archie Server	Who Should Use It
archie.ans.net	ANS network users
archie.au	Australia and other Pacific nations
archie.doc.ic.ac.uk	British Isles
archie.funet.fi	Europeans
archie.mcgill.ca	Canadians
archie.rutgers.edu	Northeastern United States
archie.sura.net	Southeastern United States
archie.unl.edu	Western United States

How To Use Archie

First, Telnet to the Archie server closest to you. For me, it's the Rutgers (northeastern U.S.) site:

```
telnet archie.rutgers.edu
```

The login id is `archie` and no password is required.

"I HATE THIS!"

Why does everyone want to use the network when I do? Sometimes I even get kicked off because the Archie is being used by so many people!

Prime time for network use is from about 9 a.m. to 3 p.m. on weekdays; any time before or after those times is faster and you are less likely to be refused access to an Archie server due to an excessive number of users.

Now that you are connected to the Rutgers University Archie site, you can use Archie to locate sites that house the Gopher software. The command is

```
prog gopher
```

The best thing about Archie is that it keeps you informed of the progress of its search. The following is displayed on your screen:

```
# Search type: sub. (stands for subject)
# Your queue position: 1 (No one ahead of me!)
# Estimated time for completion: 00:08 (That's 8 seconds!)
```

Because Archie searches through hundreds of sites looking for your keyword, it might take a long time if the server is busy. Chill, babe. Have a glass of mineral water.

If you have a GUI, you can set Archie to searching in one window while you work on something else in another window. If you don't have a GUI, you have to find something else to do to entertain yourself while Archie works.

When Archie has finished searching, a list of sites that house the Gopher software are scrolled on-screen. If there are a lot of sites, the information will scroll by too fast for you to read it. The best thing to do is to e-mail it to yourself.

To do this, wait until the information has stopped scrolling, then type

> `mail userid@node`

The information shows up in your electronic mailbox, and you can read it more carefully there, store it and read it with `vi`, or print it out.

Here are a couple of entries that resulted from an Archie search using the `prog gopher` command.

```
Host uxa.ecn.bgu.edu     (143.43.33.11)
Last updated 14:13 11 Nov 1993

    Location: /pub
        DIRECTORY      drwxr-xr-x     512 bytes  13:41  28 May
1993   gopher

Host ftp.uu.net     (192.48.96.9)
Last updated 10:01  11 Nov 1993

    Location: /networking/info-service
        DIRECTORY      drwxrwxr-x     512 bytes  22:39  27  Sep
1993  gopher

    Location: /networking/info-service/gopher/UNIX/emacs-
client
        DIRECTORY      drwxrwxr-x     512 bytes  23:51   9  Nov
1993   gopher
```

Because the Gopher software is in demand, many servers provide it. There is no way to guarantee which servers have the latest version of the software. There is, likewise, no foolproof way of telling exactly what you are getting unless the maintainer of the server has done a good job of file naming. You have to give it your best shot. The update time and date of the file will give you some idea when that file was stored or updated, but there are no guarantees.

After you have identified the best source for the software, you have to use the FTP program to connect to that site, and use the `get` command to download the necessary files to your computer. Then, you might have to use other software to uncompress those files. Finally, you have to install them on your computer. But all you've spent is your time. Or, if you're lucky, someone else's time!

Commercial Services
(Your phone bill will never be the same again)

If you've watched television or picked up a magazine lately, you know that commercial communication and information service providers are proliferating. They come in two flavors.

BUZZWORDS

E-MAIL PROVIDER

A commercial service that sells e-mail connectivity to customers. Some also offer other services, such as FAX storage, hard copy mail, and electronic data interchange.

BUZZWORDS

ON-LINE SERVICE PROVIDER

A commercial service that sells e-mail connectivity, plus other services like news groups, database searching, and catalog shopping.

There are hundreds of local and regional providers. The following list includes some of the better-known commercial Internet service providers and their phone numbers.

E-mail service providers	
✔ Advantis	800-284-5849
✔ AT&T EasyLink	800-242-6005
✔ BT North America	800-872-7654
✔ MCI Mail	800-444-6245
✔ Pacific Bell	800-423-6245
✔ SprintMail	800-736-1130

On-line service providers (including e-mail)	
✔ America Online	800-242-6005
✔ CompuServe	800-848-8199
✔ Prodigy	800-776-3449

I HATE UNIX!

	On-line service providers (including e-mail)
✔ Delphi	800-695-4005
✔ GEnie	800-638-9636

Whenever you evaluate a business service, including an on-line service, you want to obtain the best value for your money. Here are some questions to ask that will help you identify which commercial service is best for you. It costs you money to be part of such a service, and only you can decide whether it is money well spent.

Top 10 Questions To Ask When Evaluating a Service

10. How many of my first-born children will I have to sacrifice to get connected?

9. How many fast-food lunches will I have to give up to afford the monthly fee?

8. What services does my money buy me? For example, is Internet access— Gopher, Telnet, read news, FTP—included?

7. What is the per-unit charge for e-mail messages? Are blabber-mouths (blabber-fingers???) penalized by this company? If you tend toward verbosity, a service that charges by the word is not for you. Some services even go so far as to count messages longer than a specified number of words as two messages!

6. What is the per-unit charge for other types of access besides e-mail? Will I have to pay the piper whenever I Gopher? Do my connection or monthly fees include any connection time, or are you going to soak me for every minute I spend on-line?

continues

Top 10 Questions To Ask When Evaluating a Service (continued)

5. Is there a surcharge for accessing your service during peak business hours? How much extra will I pay if I prefer not to do my networking at 3:00 a.m.?

4. What other services does your company provide? (Babysitting, plant watering, term-paper writing???) How much are these services?

3. What software comes with my subscription? Or do I just get a free beach bag with my order?

2. What modem speeds are supported? (My modem has a baud rate of 9600, but my bod rate—walking on flat ground in comfortable shoes—is about 3-1/2 miles per hour.)

1. How many subscribers do you have? The more the merrier!

PART VI

Productivity Strategies—Putting UNIX To Work for You

Includes:

CHAPTER 18

Customizing Your UNIX Environment

IN A NUTSHELL

- ▼ Adding functionality
- ▼ Using aliases
- ▼ Managing processes

Are you starting to hate UNIX a little less? By now, if you've read this far, you know something about the power and flexibility of UNIX. If you've had a chance to experiment with UNIX's networking capabilities, you know that it's not only flexible, it can also be fun. It's still complex, and it's still arcane, but it's probably not as bad as you thought it was going to be. Right?

In this chapter, you gain a little added power over UNIX. You edit your resource files, to start making UNIX do things the way you want them done. If this is the only part of your life over which you have this much power, enjoy! UNIX does whatever you tell it to do, without complaining!

You learn how to change UNIX's hardest-to-remember or hardest-to-tolerate commands to something you can handle. You also learn something about UNIX processes and how to troubleshoot if things go haywire.

Adding Functionality to Your System

A number of files owned by your login id are used to control how the system acts when you are logged in. If you are using UNIX System V Release 4.2 with a C Shell, as assumed in this book, the key resource files are called .cshrc and .login. Most of this chapter deals with about the .cshrc, because it can have more influence over how UNIX behaves when you are logged in.

BUZZWORDS

.cshrc

.cshrc (pronounced just like it is spelled—dot-c-s-h-r-c) is the **C Sh**ell **r**un **c**ommand file. It contains a set of commands that UNIX can't live without, as well as commands that you have added to make your UNIX sessions tolerable.

TIP

The Korn Shell file that performs functions similar to .cshrc is named .profile or .env. Many of the commands are different from those used by the C Shell, but the idea is the same.

To see a list of all your files, including the dot files, type the following:

```
ls -a
```

BUZZWORDS

DOT FILES

Dot files, the files that begin with a period(.), are your system resource files. These are the very same files I warned you against messing around with earlier in this book. You are now on the verge of learning how to mess around with those off-limits files. You must have graduated to a high level of respect and responsibility in UNIXland!

If you are interested, use the `cat` or `vi` command to examine the contents of some of those files, just to see what they are causing to happen on your behalf. Contrary to popular belief, nothing in UNIXland happens by magic. It's all just grunt computer programming—elegant, yes, but nonetheless quite understandable.

In this section, you have a chance to make some changes to your .cshrc file (or whatever profile your particular shell uses).

Preventing Dot-File Disaster

When you edit dot files in UNIXland, you should worry about the consequences. If you are too over-confident, sooner or later you will make a mistake that you can't fix. Follow these rules when editing UNIX system files:

1. Always make a backup copy of a dot file before you start editing. For example:

```
cp .cshrc cshrc_original
```

2. Write-protect the cshrc_original file. Remember the chmod command from Chapter 14? This prevents you from accidentally erasing the only copy of the .cshrc that is known to work!! To protect you from yourself, remove all write permissions from the file by typing:

```
chmod -w cshrc_original
```

3. Now check to make sure that no one has write permission on the file:

```
ls -l cshrc_original
```

If the output of the ls -l command looks like the following, you're in business (that is, no one can do anything to the file except read it):

```
-r--r--r--  1 longacre  staff  138  Jan  14  11:02  cshrc_original
```

After you've taken these precautions, you can edit the dot file. Later, if you determine by testing that you have screwed something up, and you can't figure out how to get your dot file back the way it was in the beginning, just erase or rename it:

```
rm .cshrc
```

or

```
mv .cshrc cshrc_bad
```

Then rename the cshrc_original file back to .cshrc:

```
mv cshrc_original .cshrc
```

Even if things seem to be going well, it doesn't hurt to keep the original file around forever. It's not that big, so it takes up very little disk space, and does wonders for preserving your ability to sleep at night. Plus, someday, you may want to go back to your original configuration, or bail out a colleague who wasn't as careful as you were.

What commands can I put in my .cshrc file?

✔ The `calendar` command. If you maintain a calendar file in your home directory, the `calendar` command displays on-screen all the appointments you have entered for today's date and the next day.

✔ The system `news` command. The news of the day is displayed so you can automatically see what important new announcements have been entered. If there is a lot of news, you might want to put in the command like this:

```
news ¦ more
```

so that only one screenful at a time is displayed.

✔ Your aliases (see the section on creating aliases, later in this chapter).

continues

What commands can I put in my .cshrc file? (continued)

✔ Little love-messages to yourself, using the `echo` command. Such as:

```
echo Good morning Starshine
```

✔ Your own environment variables, which you can use in combination with other commands. For example:

```
set MORNINGMSG="Good morning Starshine"
```

```
echo $MORNINGMSG
```

causes UNIX to write `Good morning Starshine` on your screen as it's initializing all the commands in your .cshrc file.

✔ Your own environment variables used in combination with the system environment variables. For example, if dconnors enters the following two lines into her .cshrc file,

```
set MORNINGMSG="Get busy, $LOGNAME"
```

```
echo $MORNINGMSG
```

UNIX prints the following on her screen when she logs in every morning:

```
Get busy, dconnors
```

As you become more proficient with UNIX, you'll find all sorts of useful commands, scripts, and reminders to put into your .cshrc file, and, perhaps, into other files as well. Feel free to experiment. But be sure to copy the original file before you start messing around, so that you always have a way to retrace your steps and recover from any bad commands.

Causing Your New, Improved .cshrc To Kick In

One way to test your edited dot files is to log out and log back in again.

A better, faster way is to issue the **source** command by typing:

```
source .cshrc
```

This causes UNIX to reread the .cshrc file and issue all the commands. The changes take effect without your having to log out and back in again. Besides being faster, **source**-ing is better than logging out and in again, because if you've introduced a problem, you can most likely find out about it without losing the system setup you had when you began.

Commenting a File That You've Edited

It's a good idea to add comments to a file that you've edited. *Comment lines* begin with a pound sign (#). They are used to describe what the next command or set of commands is supposed to do.

For example, the following lines are in my .cshrc file:

```
# Make vi the default editor for Elm
setenv VISUAL /usr/ucb/vi
setenv EDITOR /usr/ucb/vi
```

The first line explains what the commands are trying to do. The next two lines do it.

I HATE UNIX!

"I HATE THIS!"

No one reads program comments for fun; they're supposed to be functional!

Some people let their humor run loose in the comment lines. These folks have no friends to practice their humor on. They should get a life.

EXPERTS ONLY

If you want to see what environment variables exist, issue the env command without any arguments:

```
env
```

You see a list of currently defined environment variables in the form *name=value*. The following is a list of about 1/3 of the environment variables that help to control how my UNIX account works:

```
TERM=vt102
HOME=/home/professor.hu/kitalong
SHELL=/bin/csh
USER=kitalong
VISUAL=/usr/ucb/vi
EDITOR=/usr/ucb/vi
```

When you get involved with shell programming you will make heavy use of environment variables, both system-wide ones and ones you set yourself. Check out Chapter 19 for some hints on getting started with shell scripts.

Renaming Complex Commands with Aliases

How would you like to be able to type

```
woman ls
```

when you wanted to read the manual page for the ls command? You can set it up with an *alias*.

BUZZWORDS

	ALIAS

An *alias* is a word that can be used as an abbreviation, substitute, or pseudonym for a lengthy or hateful UNIX command.

First, find out what aliases you can use, by typing:

alias

An alias list scrolls by on your screen, something like this.

```
cls clear
h   history
rd  rmdir
rm  (rm -i)
woman      man
```

Here's the syntax you need to create your own alias:

```
alias new_command "original_command"
```

So, for example, to turn man into woman, type:

```
alias woman "man"
```

Now, when you type:

```
woman ls
```

Voila! You get the man page for the `ls` command! Only now, they're called "woman pages," at least for you.

Of course there are other uses for the `alias` command. For example, if you want interactive remove (`rm -i`) set permanently on your system, you can alias it, like this:

```
alias rm "rm -i"
```

Now, when you enter the command to remove a file name UNIX prompts you for confirmation.

Or, you can make up your own special command for `rm -i` to distinguish it from `rm`, and enable you to use `rm` in the way it was intended. How about `zap`?

```
alias zap "rm -i"
```

Now if you type:

```
zap report
```

UNIX, instead of simply blowing the file away as it might do with `rm`, solicitously says:

```
rm: remove report?
```

Of course, these aliases are of very little use if you have to retype them every time you log in. So the trick is to put them in your .cshrc (c-shell resource) file, using the techniques introduced in the previous section.

Managing Processes

The way UNIX works its multitasking magic is through the miracle of processes. Imagine that you are at home. The TV is on, your spouse is in another room working on something, the dog is scratching on the sofa, dinner is cooking in the oven, and one of your kids is taking a shower (again). All of these are processes going on in your home. (This is a real moment in my home.)

Although you are aware of all the processes, most of them can take place in the background while you focus your attention on that which is most important. The process priority changes depending upon various factors. If you suddenly started to smell something unusual, you'd tick through the processes.

Household process problem probability detector

✔ Is dinner burning?

✔ Did I leave a plastic bag on the burner again?

✔ Is it the kid's new cologne?

✔ Is my spouse's project being transported to an alternate dimension?

✔ Did the sewer back up?

✔ Did a new process just start?

✔ Is the other kid building a chemical reaction in the basement?

UNIX maintains a similar level of awareness about the processes taking place within its purview. Whenever you want to, you can monitor your current processes by typing:

ps

The processes display on-screen, something like this:

```
PID TT STAT    TIME COMMAND
4345 p0 S      0:01 -csh (csh)
4464 p0 T      0:00 man ps
4465 p0 T      0:00 sh -c more -s /usr/mtu/man/cat1/ps1
4466 p0 T      0:00 more -s /usr/mtu/man/cat1/ps1
4468 p0 T      0:00 elm
4469 p0 R      0:00 ps
```

You might have many more than this, or you might have far fewer. It all depends on what you are doing.

You can get even more information if you use the -x option of the **ps** command:

```
ps -x

USER      PID %CPU  %MEM    SZ   RSS TT STAT START   TIME COMMAND
kitalong 4345  0.0   0.7    28   104 p0 S    13:20  0:01 -csh (csh)
```

I've only listed one of the processes, just to show you that the -x option lets you determine what percent of the computer's processor power or time (%CPU) and memory (%MEM) each process is using. Those numbers can be especially useful if you are having some kind of problem. For example, if the system suddenly slowed down drastically, or stopped completely, you would want to know which processes were the culprits.

Obviously, in the middle of a complete stoppage of your machine, you are not able to do anything, not even issue the **ps** command. But someone else, perhaps the system administrator, could log in remotely to your machine, check your processes and put a stop to the offending one(s).

Just a minute ago, I turned off the TV. In UNIXland, this is the equivalent of killing a process. The noise was bothering me and the process had outlived its usefulness, since no one was watching except the itchy dog, who doesn't even like *The Young and the Restless*.

In UNIXland, to get rid of a process that I no longer need, I have to use the `kill` command. But I can't just say "kill TV" (or whatever process is bothering me). In UNIXland, each process has a process id, or PID, which is displayed in the output of the `ps -aux` command.

Let's say I want to kill the `elm` process shown in the first `ps` example. It's my e-mail program, which I ran as a background process just so I could provide you with an example. Normally, it runs in the foreground, because I'm constantly working with my e-mail. To kill that process, first I would run the `ps` command to verify the process id. Then I would type:

```
kill 4468
```

As a last resort, if the `kill` command didn't do the job, I'd use the "kill it dead" command, which is `kill -9`. The syntax is the same as for the `kill` command:

```
kill -9 4468
```

I mentioned having placed the `elm` process in the background. Any process can be told to run in the background, so that it does not disturb the immediate work you are doing.

To return to that household analogy I've been belaboring, when I'm cooking dinner and reading the newspaper at the same time, the newspaper-reading is a foreground process and dinner-preparation is a background process. When it's time to start cooking the broccoli (20 minutes or so before the meatloaf is done), dinner again becomes a foreground process. I may be thinking about what *I* read in the newspaper, but even *I* cannot cook broccoli and read the newspaper at the same time, so I have to kill the newspaper-reading process, at least temporarily.

In UNIXland, if you want to run a long-running command—such as a sort of a huge database—as a background process, type an ampersand (&) immediately following the command name. In my household example, I might use the ampersand to effectively manage the multiple processes in my household by typing something like this:

```
dinner &
listen_to_scratching_dog &
read_newspaper
```

The ps command lets me check on the status of my processes. Here is the command output again:

```
PID TT STAT    TIME COMMAND
4345 p0 S       0:01 -csh (csh)
4464 p0 T       0:00 man ps
4465 p0 T       0:00 sh -c more -s /usr/mtu/man/cat1/ps1
4466 p0 T       0:00 more -s /usr/mtu/man/cat1/ps1
4468 p0 T       0:00 elm
4469 p0 R       0:00 ps
```

See that STAT column? There are six different letters that can appear there, sometimes several at once. Here's what they stand for:

R   Runnable processes

T   Stopped processes

P   Processes in page wait

D   Processes waiting for system or network resources to become available

S   Processes sleeping for a very short time

I   Idle processes (sleeping for a longer time)

From your point of view, the most important status is T. That's the letter that identifies processes you have put into the background. Sooner or later, you'll have to move them to the foreground or kill them.

Now, if I were a UNIX system, and I wanted to bring dinner-preparation to the foreground, I would type

```
fg %1
```

`fg` stands for foreground, and the number is the dinner-preparation process id, which, of course, I made up.

Have you had enough of my home-process analogy? In my opinion, it needs to go the way of the offending process—since it's outlived its usefulness, it has to be put to rest with a `kill -9` command. But do you get the idea?

When you use a GUI, each of the windows or icons on-screen corresponds to a different process. The background-to-foreground switching is usually accomplished by moving your mouse into the window to which you want to pay attention. Sometimes you also have to click the mouse to move the window from background to foreground. In the same way, killing a process can be accomplished in a GUI simply by closing or quitting the window.

Without a GUI, you only have one screen on which to make things happen, so you need the capability of switching processes in and out of UNIX's consciousness, so that they can receive the attention they deserve—when necessary. The `ps` command also helps you maintain your productivity by preventing long-running processes from taking control of your terminal.

CHAPTER 19

Sassy Shortcuts and Sneaky Scripting Techniques

IN A NUTSHELL

- ▼ Completing file names with the Escape key
- ▼ Repeating commands with history
- ▼ Saving keystrokes with wild cards
- ▼ Changing commands with the substitution symbol
- ▼ Storing command output in files
- ▼ Redirecting files as standard input
- ▼ Shell script strategies

U NIX programmers are a lazy lot—witness all the short, almost indecipherable commands, the millions of options for every command, the way they have managed to find a quick and elegant solution to any conceivable problem (except that crazy UNIX mail program).

Here are a few other little tricks to keep you C Shell users from typing your fingers to the bone—the Escape key, the `history` command, some wild cards, a cr-a-a-a-zy substitution symbol, and the standard input/output redirection symbols. (The Korn and Bourne shells have their own tricks—C Shell lovers aren't the only lazy typists in UNIXland!)

Completing File Names with the Escape Key

Don't you just hate the long file names in UNIXland? Don't you wish there was a way to avoid typing all those darn characters over and over again, especially when you make a mistake? Well, of course, there is. The mighty Escape key!

The Escape key can be used to fill out the remaining characters in a file name, if that file name is unique among the files in the current (working) directory. For example, let's say the following files and directories are stored in Ted Samson's home directory:

```
poem.4.gina
quar2
quar3
quar4
quar4_rept.dr1
steering_ctte_rept
stem_mgr_budget
zero-growth-policy
```

All of these file and directory names are pretty descriptive, but most of them are very long, and contain characters, like underscores and dashes, that can be a pain to type.

But Ted knows the Escape key secret. When he wants to work with one of these long-named files, all he has to do is type enough of the file name to distinguish the file from all the others in his directory.

For example, to edit the file named steering_ctte_rept, Ted types:

```
vi stee<Escape>
```

UNIX (well, technically, the C Shell) fills in the rest of the file name. This is called *filename completion*.

Let's try another one. If Ted wanted to change to the directory named zero-growth-policy, all he would have to type is the `cd` command followed by a `z` and the Escape key.

```
cd z<Escape>
```

Bingo! The file name is filled in and he's ready to press the Enter key and be transported into that directory.

He'd have a little more trouble with all the files beginning with the letters *quar*.

```
quar2
quar3
quar4
quar4_rept.dr1
```

To get UNIX to complete the file name for quar4_rept.dr1 so he could edit it, Ted would have to type:

```
vi quar4_<Escape>
```

If Ted simply typed:

```
vi quar4<Escape>
```

UNIX (actually the C Shell) would beep at him, because two files begin with *quar4*.

Repeating Commands with *history*

The `history` command is used to remember commands by their numbers, so you don't have to retype the whole thing. For example, Ted's command history for the previous transactions include

```
1       vi steering_ctte_rept
2       cd zero-growth-policy
3       cd ..
4       vi quar4_rept.dr1
5       history
```

Of course, the numbers may vary, but this is, after all, just an example!

Now, suppose Ted goes to lunch, and when he comes back, he wants to work some more on the steering_ctte_rept file. Instead of retyping the entire `vi steering_ctte_rept` command like I just did, Ted first types

```
history
```

to get the `history` list, and then types:

```
!1
```

to repeat command number 1, vi steering_ctte_rept.

If Ted is really averse to typing, he has undoubtedly inserted an alias into his .cshrc file—something short and sweet, like h, to take the place of the history command.

Saving Keystrokes with Wild Cards

You've already learned a little bit about wild cards. You learned somewhere earlier in this book that a splat, or asterisk (*), is used as shorthand for *any number of characters*. If Ted Samson, in the example in the previous section, types the command:

    ls q*

the resulting file list looks like this:

    quar2
    quar3
    quar4
    quar4_rept.dr1

If he types:

    ls ste*

the following file list comes up:

    steering_ctte_rept
    stem_mgr_budget

Another useful UNIX wild card is a question mark (?), which is short-hand for *any one character*. Using Ted Samson's file listing as an example again, you could type:

```
ls quar?
```

and get the following output:

```
quar2
quar3
quar4
```

Obviously, quar4_rept.dr1 no longer shows up, because more than one character comes after the *quar* part of the file name.

You can use splats and question marks in the middle of file names, and in combination with each other, to get a lot more mileage out of UNIX commands. Keep them in mind.

Changing Commands with the Substitution Symbol

If you mistype a single character in a long command, you can use the substitution character, which is a ^—that pointy-looking symbol that you can usually get by typing Shift-6. For example, suppose you wanted to edit the zero-growth-policy file, but you mistakenly typed

```
vi zero-growth-polict
```

First of all, I'd have to ask you why you were bothering to type that whole blasted command. Have you forgotten the Escape key shortcut already? Well, I'll give you the benefit of the doubt—maybe you're reading the chapter in some nonlinear order.

But all is not lost. Instead of retyping the whole command, you could simply reissue the command by using the substitution symbol to exchange y for t. Your first instinct might be to try the following:

```
^t^y
```

Before you press the Enter key, take a second look. What's wrong with this picture? Right, there is a t in *growth*, and this command only changes the first instance it encounters, so UNIX would switch the command to

```
vi zero-growyh-polict
```

thereby adding insult to injury and making your command sound like something out of Tolkien's *The Hobbit*. What would work better? Try:

```
^ct^cy
```

Would that do it? Probably.

This is a neat command if you have a lot of repetitive file management to do. For example, suppose you have written a script that converts graphics files from a format that works with your workstation graphics software to a different format that is compatible with a PC software program. The command that runs the shell script looks like this:

```
convert graphic1.rs
```

Now, you have 10 or 12 graphics files named graphic1.rs, graphic2.rs, and so on. You need to convert those files, one after another, as quickly and efficiently as possible. Instead of retyping the entire command each time, you can type it once, then use the ^ substitution character to change the numbers.

```
convert graphic1.rs
^1^2
^2^3
^3^4
```

You can probably write a shell script that automates the process even more. Obviously, if you convert a lot of graphics files, it would be worth your time to write that script—but not for a mere 10 or 12 conversions.

Storing Command Output in Files

The whole idea of standard input and output is confusing. What is the standard output of the ls command? Well, it's a list of all your files in the current directory. The standard place for standard output to appear is on-screen. If you want the standard output to go someplace else other than the screen, you *redirect* it, as we did when we instructed UNIX to place the output of a command into a file. For example, if you type:

```
man ls > list.doc
```

the output of the man ls command is stored as a file named list.doc.

Redirecting Files as Standard Input

The opposite of standard output is standard input. The natural place for standard input to come from is the keyboard. It is used productively in shell scripting, but another great use for it is enclosing files in e-mail messages.

Let's say you and good old Ted Samson are going on a business trip. You were in charge of making the travel arrangements, so when the travel agent calls you with the plans, you naturally want Ted to have the latest scoop. Use vi to type the itinerary into a file named, of all things, *itinerary*. Then send Ted e-mail, using the following command to enclose the itinerary in the message:

```
mail samson < itinerary
```

Soon, Ted will be as well informed as you are about the business trip.

Obviously, there are many more sophisticated uses for all of these short-cuts than the ones I've described here. But I'm not going to burden you with them. If you need more sophisticated solutions, you'll find them for yourself.

Simply Sneaky Shell Script Strategies

If you take a little bit of time to learn some simple C Shell programming, you can save yourself much time in the long run. Throughout this book, I've shared commands with you that would make dynamite sections of shell scripts; at the very least, some of those commands could be used to automate mindless and boring tasks that you are required to do.

Commands and functions for useful shell script instructions	
✔ grep	Systematically goes through bunches of files and locates the characters that you specify
✔ find	Locates specific files for you
✔ >	Redirects the standard output of a command into a file
✔ <	Redirects a file to the standard input of a command
✔ ¦	Redirects the standard output of a command to the standard input of another command; no need to save the output as a file before redirecting
✔ echo	Causes something to print to the screen
✔ set	Sets an environment variable
✔ read	Asks for some input from the keyboard
✔ wc	Counts the number of words in a file
✔ wc -l	Counts the number of lines in a file
✔ wc -c	Counts the number of characters in a file
✔ sleep	Waits for a specified number of seconds

Imagine that you find yourself repeating a series of commands over and over, in a predictable sequence. If you want to, you can automate that sequence of commands by creating an executable shell script. For example, let's say that you are entering a large number of client addresses into a data file named address.data. You find it useful and very satisfying to know how many total entries are in the file. Type the following to find this out:

```
wc -l address.data
```

If you wanted to automate this little two-step process just a tad, write a shell script called count that includes the following line:

```
cat address.data ¦ wc -l
```

Once you've created the program file named count, use the chmod command to change the file mode so that it can be executed:

```
chmod u+x count
```

Now you're ready to count how many lines the file contains. Type:

```
count
```

at the UNIX system prompt, and your line count is echoed on-screen.

You could fancy it up a bit by adding a couple of lines, like this:

```
echo "Congratulations! You have entered"
cat address.data ¦ wc -l
echo "addresses already!!"
```

Maybe you've had enough of C Shell scripts and you never want to see or hear of them again. But if you want to become an expert shell scripter, you'll have no trouble finding yourself a good book, such as Que's *Using UNIX*, Special Edition. *I Hate UNIX!* is not the place to learn the finer points of shell scripting!

PART VII

Quick and Dirty Dozens

Includes:

I HATE UNIX

Quick and Dirty Dozens

IN A NUTSHELL

▼ 12 Things To Do Next

▼ Tons of Things To Know About
System Administration

▼ 12 Ways To Use the Network
for Fun and Profit

12 Things To Do Next

1. Practice with your GUI.

If you have a graphical user interface (GUI), you never run out of new things to learn about it. Here are a few things to explore:

✔ How do you put a background picture on to your screen? You can try the company logo, a mug shot of your sweetie or your hero or your favorite cartoon character, a picture of the moon that changes as the month progresses, or your latest sales graph.

✔ Does it do sound? If so, how? Can you include sound in a mail message or attach it to a print document?

✔ Can you change the icons with your file manager? If you wanted to create a little graphic to attach to all folders that contain financial information, how would you do it?

Read the documentation that came with your GUI. If you don't feel like reading all the documentation, you can be sure that there's an overview booklet or chapter. Read that. Find one new thing that you didn't know and learn how to do it.

2. Ask your guru an *intelligent* question.

Gone are the days when companies pay programmers to sit around and program. In most companies, everyone—even the most introverted, linear, single-minded programmer type—has to work as a team with others and answer questions when a user needs help.

I HATE UNIX!

When you have to ask a question, keep in mind that your guru is bound to ask *you* some or all the following questions:

✔ Did you read the manual (man pages)? Gurus think the man pages are the best thing in the world. They expect that you have at least tried to find the answer to your question yourself by looking it up. In the next section, you learn about the keyword option of the man command, which you can use if you don't know which command you need to do the job.

✔ What were you doing when the problem occurred? Don't say, "Nothing, I was just sitting there." The guru will not believe you. Computer problems rarely happen spontaneously.

✔ Did you do anything different this time? Even a tiny, seemingly insignificant difference in your routine can make a huge amount of difference to a computer. So try to think back to what was different about the situation today.

The guru may ask other questions, too. Gurus are people; each one is different. What they have in common is that they know more about UNIX than you do.

One thing to keep in mind is that the guru probably does not want to know what you think the problem is. He or she prefers to know what symptoms you observed. Like a child with a fever, so is a computer with a problem. Many things can cause a fever and a computer problem; you want to rule out the obvious ones first, then get to the more esoteric ones.

3. **Find a new command by using the `man -k` command.**

If you can't remember a particular command, or you want to know if there's a command that does a particular function related to directories, you can use the `-k` option of the `man` command:

```
man -k directory ¦ more
```

Unlike the straight `man` command, `man -k` doesn't automatically go to more or page mode, so you need to pipe the standard output of the `man -k` command to the `more` command.

A list appears on-screen that includes commands like the following:

`mkdirhier (1)`	Makes a directory hierarchy
`du (1V)`	Displays the number of disk blocks used per directory or file
`ls`	Lists the contents of a directory
`mkdir`	Makes a directory

The actual list I got when I issued the `man -k` directory command included about four times as many commands as this—all the commands, in fact, that have the word *directory* in their man page short description.

This is a good way to find new commands, which you can then read all about with the regular `man` command.

I HATE UNIX!

CAUTION

When you learn new commands this way, be sure that you are clear on what the outcome of issuing the command is. Sometimes commands can cause weird responses that you could not have predicted.

4. **Issue the new command you find, just to see what happens.**

Well, don't just do this without contemplating it for a few minutes. Please be sure that your new toy isn't destructive, and make sure that it's meant to be used by ordinary UNIX users, not just by someone in authority!

How to engage in safe ex(perimenting) with new UNIX commands

✔ Read the man page carefully, including between the lines.

✔ If there's some part of the man page description that you don't understand, find out what it means.

✔ When you're reasonably confident that it's an OK command that won't kill you or anyone around you, try it!

5. **Look at your system files—and change them if you dare.**

You've already learned about changing your system files. Obviously, they're your system files and you can change them if you want. Just remember another set of rules for *safe ex*:

✔ Always make copies of key files before you change them. This gives you an escape if you screw something up.

✔ Always test all your changes. Use the `source` command and take careful note of what happens, including any error messages. In addition, even if you think you have the system file working the way it should, pay close attention to what you're doing for the next day or two. Keep in mind that if strange things happen, it may be as a result of your changes.

✔ Don't make more than one change at a time. Change something, test it, make sure it's working, then go on to the next change. This helps you isolate problems that come up.

✔ Document your changes by inserting comments (lines beginning with a #) in the file. It's not a bad idea to initial and date those comment lines, too. Take responsibility for the system updates you make!

6. **Organize your UNIX file system to match your office file system.**

After you've been working with your new UNIX system for a while, you will find that files have proliferated and you can't find anything. You might want to take a couple of hours some afternoon and invent a nice, logical organization for all of your stuff.

Advantages of a good file system organization

✔ Makes it easier for you to decide what to do with new files.

✔ Makes it easier for you to find files once you've done something with them.

✔ If you suddenly get sick and can't come to work for a while, anyone who is familiar with your office set-up is able to find things in your computer set-up.

A good, intuitive way to arrange your UNIX files is to mirror the organization of the physical files in your office. After all, why re-invent the wheel—unless, of course, your office file system is in a shambles! If so, then you can devise a great, logical, intuitive system in your home directory and mirror it in your office!

Let's say you have four file cabinets in your office, and each has four drawers. That's sixteen labeled file drawers. Here's a foolproof process for making your UNIX files emulate the organization of your physical files.

Organizing your UNIX files to match your office files

✔ Use the UNIX `mkdir` command to create sixteen directories within your home directory, giving them names that correspond to your sixteen file drawers.

✔ Use the `mv` command to move all of your existing files into one of the directories.

✔ If necessary, create subdirectories within each main directory, to improve the organization further. You can even create subdirectories within the subdirectories, but don't get too deep.

✔ Then, whenever you create a document or receive some e-mail, you can file it on the computer the way you would file it in your office file cabinets.

---

7. **Look at someone else's files.**

Remember how to change to someone else's home directory if they are on the same file system as you are?

```
cd ~username
```

Recall that to change to Ted Samson's home directory, you type:

```
cd ~samson
```

You don't want to get in the habit of perusing other people's files, but there are a couple of good reasons for doing so:

✔ To see what kind of organizational scheme they have devised for their files and directories

✔ If you are working on a project with them, to copy, link, or read certain files

✔ To drop off files in their Incoming directory

✔ To help them with a problem they might be having

If you can't claim one of the above reasons, or another equally valid one, then stay out of other people's files. You don't go into coworkers' offices and snoop around, do you? Don't answer that!

8. Compress your files to free up some disk space.

The compress command in UNIX System V Release 4.2 makes it really easy to save disk space. Compressing large files that you rarely use may not be necessary, but it is the polite thing to do.

The compress command compacts the file and appends an extension of .Z to the file name. Here is the command syntax:

```
compress filename
```

To compress a file called empl.hndbk.90, a 200-page document that has been superseded by a 1994 version, type:

compress empl.hndbk.90

To tell how much compression is taking place, you can use the compress command's -v option:

    compress -v empl.hndbk.90

If you were to list all the files after executing the compress command, among those files you would see is

    empl.hndbk.90.Z

You might want to use the ls -l command before and after doing the compression, just to see for yourself the difference in size after compression.

If you ever need to use the file again—maybe to reinstate a policy that had been in effect in 1990, but was disbanded in 1994—you can get back the original 1990 handbook with the uncompress command, again, using the -v option if you want:

    uncompress -v empl.hndbk.90.Z

If you do a lot of FTP-ing from sites all around the Internet, you'll encounter some .Z files—remember, we mentioned this command back in Chapter 17. This same uncompress command can be used to uncompress those files so you can read them.

9. **Find out who else is logged in.**

There are three little commands that you can use to see who is logged in, what they are doing, and perhaps a few notes about them, such as who they are and what they think about life.

You already learned the `who` command, all the way back in Chapter 1. Just in case you've forgotten, here's how it works:

```
who
```

And here's what the response looks like:

```
kitalong ttyp0   Nov 29 06:10  (trmsrv06.tc.mtu.)
```

It tells you everyone who is logged in—in this case, just one person—what kind of terminal is being used, the date and time of the login, and the location of the terminal the person is using. In the above example, I was logged in remotely (I rarely go to the office at 6 a.m.!).

10. **Find out what people are doing with the server.**

The `w` command, although shorter than `who`, gives you a little more information about the people who are logged in. Type:

```
w
```

and you see something like the following:

```
11:15am  up 15 days, 23:22,   1 user,  load average: 0.05, 0.00, 0.00
User     tty       login@   idle   JCPU   PCPU   what
dconnors ttyp0    11:01am           8      1    mail
```

The first line tells something about the server: How long it has been running continuously (15 days), how many users are on it, and what the average work load on the server is. It's not that interesting to anyone other than the system administrator.

The next lines, though, tell you about individual logged-in users and their activities. The `idle` column tells you how many minutes it's been since that person typed a command. To tell you the truth, I have no idea (nor do I care) what the JCPU and PCPU columns mean, although I suppose I could find out if I read the man page. Finally, the `what` column tells you the most recent command that user issued. This person is reading her mail.

11. **Finger someone's id.**

Finally, the `finger` command—as questionable as it sounds—is a perfectly legitimate and not at all objectionable way to get a report on one or all users of the UNIX system.

If you type

```
finger
```

without any arguments at all, you get a brief report on all logged-in users, including the names of the terminal ports they are using, their log-in times, the time in minutes since a command was issued, and other information.

A more interesting use of the `finger` command is to give it someone's id as an argument, to get more detailed information about that particular person. If you type

```
finger dconnors
```

for example, you might see the following:

```
Login name: dconnors          In real life: Debra C. Connors
Directory: /home/sales.server/dconnors      Shell: /bin/csh
Last login Wed Dec 29 11:01 on ttyp0
New mail received Thu Dec 30 14:28:33 1993;
  unread since Wed Dec 29 11:06:14 1993
Project: Increasing sales 20% in 1994
Plan:
Dec 29 2 p.m. sales meeting, conf room c
Dec 30 4:30 p.m. haircut
```

If you finger yourself, chances are you are lacking some of the information you see about Debra. That's because Debra has filled out .project and .plan files in her home directory.

You can use vi to put anything you want into these files. Apparently, Debra likes her goals to be visible to anyone, so her .project file contains that information.

Debra uses the .plan file to announce her appointments to the world. This can be done in a couple of ways.

✔ First thing in the morning, update your calendar file. Remember the calendar file? We learned about it in Chapter 11.

✔ Run the calendar command and redirect its output to the .plan file, thereby creating an updated .plan.

```
calendar > .plan
```

Another way to do this is to put a little sequence of commands in your .login or .cshrc or .profile file, so that it automatically happens

when you log in. Then, your job is to update your calendar before you log out every day, so that the next day when you log in, the new updates are reflected in your .plan.

Here's a simple sequence of commands to insert in your .cshrc file:

```
#Put standard output of calendar command into .plan file
unset noclobber
calendar > .plan
set noclobber
#That's it
```

The `noclobber` command keeps you from over-writing existing files. So we `unset noclobber` (a double negative that would make Miss Rheingold, my 4th grade teacher, faint dead away!). Then we run the `calendar` command, and blithely write it to the .plan file, thereby destroying anything that was previously in the .plan file. Finally, we reset `noclobber`, so we won't accidentally clobber files we really need.

Obviously, `finger` is used with great results by your system administrator, but, unless you are that person, you can just `finger` for fun.

12. **Learn another dozen things about your UNIX system.**

There's no end to the number of new things you can find to hate about UNIX. No matter how long you have been working with it, you never exhaust all of its possibilities. But, you can get along just fine in UNIXland without knowing more than a fraction of what UNIX has to offer. So don't worry, be happy!

Tons of Things To Know about System Administration

1. **What does a system administrator do?**

   In general, a system administrator is in charge of the care and feeding of a dozen or more types of hardware, including computers, printers, scanners, plotters, disk drives, keyboards, and monitors. In addition, system administrators install and maintain software and fix things when they break.

   There are at least five categories of tasks system administrators must know or learn how to do (the next five items explain these categories). The smaller your operation, the more of them you have to do if you are the system administrator. Larger shops may have specialists for some of these areas, but none of them is out of the realm of possibility for the system administrator.

2. **System administrators deal with people's computer accounts.**

   This is the type of general account stuff that system administrators are responsible for handling on a regular basis:

   ✔ Adding new users.

   ✔ Backing up everyone's data, usually every day. This can be done automatically, by means of a shell script or backup program, after everyone, including the system administrator, goes home at night.

   ✔ Checking to make sure the backups worked properly.

✔ Recovering files that users accidentally erased or mangled. This is why backups are done.

✔ Answering questions. A few people will have the foresight to think up questions during normal business hours. More often, though, people will accost you at home, at parties, in grocery lines, and at fine restaurants.

3. **System administrators handle hardware.**

Handling hardware means thinking about and knowing how to do a wide variety of separate and distinct tasks. If you want to get into system administration, think about all of these issues:

✔ Installing new hardware, including computers, terminals, keyboards, scanners, printers, plotters, disk drives, radios, microwave ovens, VCRs, wireless phones, and answering machines. If you understand technology, you are asked to help with all kinds of high-tech installations.

✔ Moving existing hardware. Sometimes this is done at the whim of the user—every company has at least one restless soul who is always rearranging his office. Sometimes the move is your idea. As you know, UNIX systems, especially net-worked ones, cannot be moved by just anyone. They can't even be turned on and off by just anyone.

✔ Rearranging furniture to accommodate new or rearranged hardware, or new or deranged colleagues.

✔ Making hardware work. This can entail everything from add-ing toner to printers to bringing the computer back up when it goes down. And it *will* go down.

✔ Optimizing users' access to hardware. Remember, a few chapters back, we described an office wellness program that involved users being assigned default access to printers half a building away? This might not be an optimal solution for you. You have to fix it.

4. **System administrators get to play with software.**

For many people, this can even be fun. Being responsible for software administration also includes loading and debugging programs and altering setups to accommodate the endlessly-changing needs of users, so beware! Here are some of the common tasks:

✔ Ensuring that there is enough disk space to accommodate a new software package, and enough memory to run it.

✔ Installing software.

✔ Making software work.

✔ Maintaining appropriate access to software, so that it's available to those who need it.

✔ Making sure everyone can print files created with the new software.

✔ Answering questions about how to use the software, even though installing it really doesn't require knowing how to use it.

5. **System administrators have to think about systems as a whole.**

If you aren't used to thinking in a global sense, this facet of system administration may be the most troubling for you. You are responsible for all of these tasks:

- ✔ Installing updates to the operating system (for example, when System V Release 4.3 or 5.9 or 6.8 comes out).

- ✔ Making sure things are secure. Blocking "holes" through which hackers can enter the system.

- ✔ Making sure there is enough memory and disk space to run things properly. Continuously reconfiguring things to maximize memory and free up disk space.

- ✔ Monitoring network traffic and trying to ensure that everything flows smoothly.

- ✔ Noticing where the system is overloaded. Making it work better even when it is overloaded.

- ✔ Rebooting the system when it goes down.

- ✔ Bringing the system down at regularly scheduled (and often very inconvenient, for you) times, so that you can fix annoying little problems.

- ✔ Designing and writing specs for new systems or system upgrades.

6. **System administrators get to deal with people, many of whom hate UNIX.**

This task is probably worse than it sounds. Once you get to know—and maybe even like—a system, and you've figured out its quirks and bugs, you want everybody else to work well with it, too. This is almost impossible. If you want to try it, just keep in mind that you have to do all these things:

✔ Know lots of little commands that people can use to get things to happen.

✔ Communicate these little commands to people for the first, tenth, or hundredth time.

✔ Attend meetings for the first, tenth, or hundredth time.

✔ Explain how things work for the first, tenth, or hundredth time.

✔ Soothe panicked users for the first, tenth, or hundredth time.

7. **System administrators get burned out.**

As you might guess, burnout is a serious problem for system administrators. There is rarely a time when everything is going smoothly. There are system administrators who focus all their attention on system integrity and optimization, and others who spend the majority of their time making sure that the users of the system are satisfied. Somewhere in the middle is a happy medium between happy users and a secure, smoothly-running system. The system administrator has to set some bounds, because he or she may be the only person who understands the extent to which a happy computer leads to happy users.

8. **System administrators must understand the difference between the shell and UNIX.**

In this book, I've adopted a rather cavalier attitude toward UNIX. In fact, I may have given the impression that I don't know the difference between UNIX and the shell. To people who know UNIX well, this is sacrilege.

I risk being excommunicated by the UNIX faithful, because I remember very well what it was like to be a beginning UNIX user. I've only been using UNIX for a couple of years, and I know that to most beginning users, the shell is UNIX and UNIX is the shell. It takes a long time and much concentration to start caring about whether you are dealing with UNIX or the shell at any given moment. If you want to be a system administrator, however, you better develop this level of caring, and unlearn some of the things I've told you in this book.

System administrators are obliged to know the difference between UNIX and the shell. Not only do they know the difference, but, believe it or not, they develop a reasoned opinion about which shell (Korn, Bourne, or C) is better. They may even argue with others about the relative merits of different UNIX shells.

9. **Are you system administrator material?**

Throughout this book, I've hinted that someone, perhaps you, must take on the responsibility of administering UNIX systems. That's because UNIX systems don't administer themselves. Anytime you have several people using one system, a certain amount of tweaking is warranted, to make sure one person isn't hogging all the disk space, making the printers act up, or invading people's privacy.

I HATE UNIX!

Sometimes, the person who knows the most about computers gets saddled with this task, either because they volunteered, or because their level of expertise makes them the logical choice, or even because no one likes them. If you have been chosen for this honor, you need to ask yourself some questions.

Half-a-dozen qualities of a good system administrator

✔ *Computer competence.* If you are very well-versed in some mainframe or networked computer system, you will do OK as a system administrator in UNIXland. So, have you been a mainframe system programmer or software installer and administrator? Have you installed and maintained PC LAN hardware and software? Do you have a relatively recent computer science, management information systems, or other computer-related college degree?

✔ *Linear, logical, systematic work style.* A system administrator's objective is to enforce policies and procedures that maximize both system performance and user access. This sometimes requires balancing conflicting priorities, yet doing so in a reasoned, professional manner, without panicking when things get hairy.

✔ *Ability to keep a secret.* System administrators have access to all aspects of a system, including users' mail, private files, and data repositories like payroll systems. They have unprecedented access to office gossip, but they can't reveal anything, because they shouldn't know it.

✔ *Ability to become super-user in a responsible manner.* The person who assumes *root*, or *super-user identity* on a computer system has read, write, and execute permission on everything that is stored on that system. They are, in effect, the one true owner of that system. Forget about withholding permission from super-user. Super-user can

trash secure files in a single bound. It's a big responsibility, and not one to be taken lightly.

✔ *Ability to decipher computer documentation.* Remember those manual pages? Are you interested in reading stuff like that every day for the rest of your natural life? Computer documentation is notoriously difficult to read; after all, where do you think the saying, "If all else fails, read the instructions" came from?

✔ *Ability to simultaneously pay attention to both the big picture and its details.* Can you, with a little bit of tenacity, detect subtle causal connections between the big picture and the details that compose the big picture? If so, then you will make a dynamite system administrator.

10. **What to do if you can't get out of being a system administrator.**

In this time of downsizing, the reality is that you may lose your job if you express unwillingness to assume additional responsibilities. Heck, you may lose your job even if you volunteer to do everyone else's job as well as your own, and take a pay cut to boot! In short, learning system administration might be a necessity. If so, here are some suggestions; insist on as many of these as you can.

12 things to demand if you are asked to be system administrator

✔ Get your boss to reassign some of your normal duties to someone else, so that you have adequate time to devote to system administration. Review the list of job tasks outlined earlier for ammunition.

continues

I HATE UNIX!

✔ Negotiate a raise in pay. Whatever you make, it won't be enough.

✔ Take some courses or attend a seminar. Good topics include vendor seminars on the particular hardware and software you will be installing and maintaining, general UNIX training, courses in programming (especially in the C programming language, which is different from the C shell), courses or workshops in shell script development, general courses in structured programming. With the proliferation of UNIX-based systems, there is a growing availability of such training, although if you don't live in a city or near a college, you may have to travel to participate.

✔ Read printed stuff. A number of UNIX journals are now available, including hardware-specific ones. There are even a few good books on the subject of system administration—try looking under UNIX in the *Books in Print* listings at your local library or bookstore.

✔ Read on-line stuff. The readnews capability of your computer system puts you in touch with other UNIX system administrators, some of whom are novices like you. Mailing lists are also "out there" on the network; ask around and you'll find them.

✔ Find a master system administrator and become his or her apprentice. One of the best ways to learn system administration is to do it under the patient and knowledgeable tutelage of an experienced system administrator. Get your boss to authorize you to spend a certain number of hours joined at the hip with the person who does this work, either at your company or at another company.

✔ Do what you can and contract out the rest. Maybe the size or stability or consistency of your company's UNIX installation doesn't require much maintenance. Maybe you can hire a senior or

graduate computer science student from the local university to do some of the more technical programming work for you. Or maybe you can contract with the vendor who sets up your system.

✔ Buy a GUI-based system administration toolkit. Hire a specialist to configure those tools for you and to come in periodically to make updates. You can then administer by pointing and clicking.

✔ Set good, sound, defensible policies for how things are done, and then stick to your guns if it's reasonable.

✔ Listen to your users. Be assertive, be a stickler for policies and procedures, but stay open to valid reasons to change your mind.

✔ Document everything you do.

✔ Know your physical and system limitations. Don't let yourself be taken advantage of. Beware of burnout.

There are ways to get things done without doing them yourself, and ways to get trained to do them without spending much money. You need to explore a variety of alternatives before committing yourself to an eternity of system administering.

12 Ways To Use the Network for Fun and Profit

1. Profit? Can I make a profit?

It depends on the opinion of the person or entity paying for your network connection. If you are paying for it yourself, no problem.

If your company is paying for it, your connection is already making a profit for the company. Can you make a personal profit from it? You better ask before you try. Maybe you can arrange to rent some time on the company's connection.

If a non-profit organization is paying for it, watch out. Those are our tax dollars at work! Some non-profit organizations arrange for their employees to rent computer and network time.

But why fool around with renting someone else's time, when you can buy your own access with one of the commercial services mentioned in Chapter 17?

2. **Travel the world without leaving your office.**

The first time I used Telnet to "go" to a library in London, England to look up some materials, I felt as if I had been transported into a fairy tale. It wasn't as exciting as a magic carpet ride, but the thought of being able to poke around in the card catalog at a library thousands of miles away really blew my hair back.

In a few years, it will be possible to access, not only the card catalog entry, but the texts themselves in electronic format, as well as images, musical selections, and audio recordings. What if, when you needed inspiration, you could call up a video of Martin Luther King's famous "I Have a Dream" speech from a library archive in Alabama and view it on your computer screen? What if third graders studying koala bears could Telnet to a zoology lab in Australia and view footage of koalas shot only yesterday? What if high school physics students could talk to the astronauts aboard a space lab?

The hardware and software needed to do these things aren't quite here yet. But the time is coming, and you're on the forefront. By learning how to navigate the Internet, you're laying the proper groundwork, so that when the capabilities are here, you are ready!

3. **Look up a book in the Library of Congress.**

Either access the Library of Congress through the Gopher system, or

```
telnet dra.com
```

and follow the instructions.

4. **Send the President some e-mail.**

The president and vice-president of the United States have electronic mail addresses! They are:

President@whitehouse.gov

VicePresident@whitehouse.gov

You may not get a personalized response from the USA's fearless leaders, but you at least get an acknowledgment. This is progress!

5. **Find out what NASA is up to.**

You can read frequently-updated news briefs on NASA activities by using the `finger` command. Remember? It was described earlier, as a way to find out about people on your system. You can also use it to check out other systems. Here's how to get to the NASA news briefs by way of the `finger` command:

```
finger nasanews@space.mit.edu
```

6. Join an e-mail list (or a dozen lists).

An e-mail list is an on-line discussion group made up of people who share an interest in a particular subject. Often, the best way to find out about e-mail lists may be to hear about them from friends, colleagues, or members of your professional society. However, compendia of e-mail lists are stored on the Internet.

A list of BITNET discussion lists is available by typing:

```
ftp lilac.berkeley.edu
```

When you get there, use `anonymous` as your login name, and, for a password, type in your e-mail address. Then type: **cd netinfo**

To get a file listing type:

```
ls
```

To change to the binet directory type:

```
cd bitnet
```

Use the `get` command for any file that sparks your interest.

listserv.groups is a good one. At the beginning of this file, you find detailed instructions on how to subscribe to the listed discussion groups.

Information on how to subscribe to BITNET lists is also stored at the lilac.berkeley.edu site.

7. Plan a wedding.

If you have a PC and are getting married soon, use FTP to get a shareware wedding planner program. If you don't have a PC, ask for one as an early wedding present so you can use it to plan the wedding!

SHAREWARE

Shareware is computer software that anyone can obtain and use. The agreement is that if you like the software, you will send the creator a modest license fee. Share-ware developers include their names and mailing addresses with their software, so honest users can comply with the fee payment.

To get the shareware wedding planner, type:

```
ftp wuarchive.wustl.edu
```

Login as anonymous and for a password, type your e-mail address.

Then type:

```
cd mirrors/msdos/database
```

To locate the wedding software, try typing ls *wed* once you're in the database directory.

Because the software is "zipped," change to binary file transfer mode by typing binary; then, use the get command to download the software to your home computer. You have to "unzip" it once you get it back home.

I HATE UNIX!

8. Play around on a freenet.

Just as the CARL system is a preview of what libraries of the future will look like, so the Cleveland Freenet is a tantalizing sneak peek at future information repositories. To get to the Cleveland Freenet, use the Telnet program:

```
telnet freenet-in-a.cwru.edu
```

or

```
telnet freenet-in-b.cwru.edu
```

or

```
telnet freenet-in-c.cwru.edu
```

TIP

This is a very busy site. Your best bet is early in the morning or late at night. If you don't get in right away, don't despair. Keep trying. It is well worth the wait.

When you get there, follow the instructions on-screen. Feel free to explore at your leisure, as a guest. If you like it, become a registered member and take advantage of all the available services.

One of the things collected at the Cleveland Freenet is a list of recent Supreme Court decisions. You find them in the Courthouse.

9. Grab a list of UNIX books.

Now that you have been exposed to UNIXland, you undoubtedly want to learn more. You'll find that a new UNIX book comes out every day, many of them from Que. A guy named Mitch Wright

312

maintains a list of UNIX books on-line—if you want to look there to see what's on his list, type the following:

```
ftp ftp.rahul.net
```

Login as anonymous and as a password, enter your e-mail id.

Then type:

```
cd pub/mitch/YABL
```

Switch to binary file transfer mode by typing:

```
binary
```

Then type:

```
get yabl.Z
```

When you get the file back to your home directory, type:

```
uncompress yabl.Z
```

and then read the file, which is named yabl, with vi.

10. **Grab some UNIX information.**

A UNIX reference manual is available by anonymous FTP.

```
ftp ucselx.sdsu.edu
```

Login as anonymous and type:

```
cd pub/doc/general
```

ls the files; you might try typing ls *un* so you just get the UNIX documents. Then get the files you want. The names are fairly self-explanatory.

11. **Dig up a new recipe.**

One of the favorite topics of conversation on the Internet, as everywhere else, is food. When people exchange recipes on the Internet, it's a simple matter to collect those recipes and make them available forevermore in electronic form. You'll never again be at a loss for what to cook.

```
ftp gatekeeper.dec.com
```

login as anonymous and for a password, type your e-mail id.

Then type:

```
cd pub/recipes
```

Use the ls command to get a list of recipes. There are a lot of them, organized by the title of the dish. If you have an idea what you want to cook, use wild cards along with the ls command:

```
ls *chick*

ls *beef*

ls *mex*
```

ls *spin* (for some reason, spinach dishes abound here!)

```
ls *choc*
```

12. Learn about a dozen more things to do

You've just scratched the surface. Keep on exploring, keep your ear to the ground for the names of FTP or public Telnet sites, travel the Gopher tunnels. You find all sorts of things—more every day. Share this knowledge with your friends, and get them to share their knowledge with you. It's time to stop hating UNIX, and start making it work for you.

Index

Symbols

A

F

G

Q

R

I HATE UNIX!

INDEX

X-Y-Z